# Finding New Ideas in Old Ones
Ten Years of Atlas Network's Leonard Liggio Lecture Series

### Edited by Brad Lips

ATLAS NETWORK

Finding New Ideas in Old Ones
Ten Years of Atlas Network's Leonard Liggio Lecture Series

Copyright © 2023 by Atlas Network
Atlas Network gratefully acknowledges the creators of the enclosed lectures for granting permission to reproduce their works in this volume.

All rights reserved.
Printed in the United States of America.

Edited by Brad Lips
Copyedited by Dara Ekanger
Book and Cover Design by Colleen Cummings

ISBN: 979-8-9868088-0-2
Ebook ISBN: 979-8-9868088-1-9
Library of Congress Control Number: 2022915461

Atlas Network
Two Liberty Center
4075 Wilson Blvd.
Suite 310
Arlington, VA 22203
www.AtlasNetwork.org

# TABLE OF CONTENTS

Foreword .................................................................................................5
By Tom G. Palmer

Introduction: Building the Liberty Movement..........................................9
By Brad Lips

The Beauty of Liberty and the Power of Saying No .............................17
By James Otteson

Market Society: The Tiny Tim Defense..................................................29
By John Tomasi

Restoring Our Republican Constitution.................................................39
By Randy E. Barnett

The Classical Liberal Tradition of Sound Money...................................59
By Lawrence H. White

Rediscovering Political Ideals................................................................77
By David Schmidtz

The Future of Regulation:
What We Can Learn from the Past........................................................89
By Hon. Douglas H. Ginsburg

Context, Continuity, and Truth:
Theory, History, and Political Economy ...............................................105
By Peter Boettke

Once More: Liberalism and Some Problems
of Historical Transmission between the Generations.........................123
By Lenore T. Ealy

Preserving Liberalism amid Emergencies ..........................................143
By Gabriel Calzada Álvarez

Remembering Leonard Liggio.............................................................177
Organized by Brad Lips

About Atlas Network ...........................................................................207

# FOREWORD
*By Tom G. Palmer*

Leonard P. Liggio may have been the kindest person I have ever known. Part of his kindness was his generosity. Leonard was always ready with a suggestion for reading, for research, for a paper, for a thesis, for a dissertation, for a project. He encouraged and never berated. He read at least one major book per day, often while watching a hockey game and eating pretzels, and the next morning he would share some of the amazing—and often amusing and counterintuitive—things he had read the night before. He could discuss and share insights about the medieval law merchant in Europe, the distinction between Daoists and Legalists in Chinese history, the complex regulation of Albanian blood feuds by the Canon of Lekë Dukagjini, the history of slave revolts in Brazil, or New Zealand's Treaty of Waitangi.

At a student conference some four decades ago, several of us asked him what impact the educational system of the Mandarins had on the development of the Chinese state and timed his response. It was a half-hour lesson in itself. When he would lecture in Europe or Latin America, he typically began with an inspiring story about the struggle for liberty that was drawn from the history of the city or town where he was teaching, almost always to the astonishment of the local audience, most of whom did not know their own civic history as well as Leonard did. He endeared himself to generations of students with his encyclopedic knowledge, his patience, and his encouragement.

Leonard was many things to many people, and many beneficiaries of his philanthropy and generosity did not know of his intellectual and scholarly activities, but it is the latter that this collection commemorates, in the hope that his generosity will continue to benefit the liberty movement for many years.

When I was studying at St. John's College in Annapolis, Maryland, I discovered in the library the writings of the French liberal historian Augustin Thierry, which had last been signed out roughly a hundred years before. I was very excited by my discovery, and so I sent a letter about what I was reading to Leonard, who responded with enthusiasm about my interest and then proceeded to explain to me both the important insights that Thierry had and some of the errors that that pioneering scholar of historical documentation had made. He encouraged me to study other French liberal thinkers, as well as the baleful impact that some of those ideas had when misappropriated and misunderstood by Karl Marx, who stirred them into the farrago that came to be known as Marxism. His suggestions for further reading were invaluable to me, as they were to so many others.

Leonard helped those of us who had the privilege to know him to see connections between ideas and events that we had not seen. These lectures continue in that tradition. Leonard believed that a historian who read no economics would be a poor historian, and vice versa. And similarly for philosophers and sociologists and students and scholars of geography and law and literature and art and other disciplines.

I used to say that Leonard had a thousand-year plan for liberty and that, even though the rest of us couldn't see all that he saw, we trusted that he had it sorted out. His encouragement of original thinkers and serious scholars, including those whose lectures in his honor are collected here, is surely an essential part of that plan. Leonard continues to encourage us to think deeply and to read widely; to share ideas and books; to appreciate the many stories of liberty embedded in every city, country, nation, and civilization; to ask ourselves hard questions; and to challenge ourselves and our colleagues to do better. The lectures in this collection live up to Leonard's legacy. They don't merely instruct; they invite us to think and definitely to read further. Whether humans will enjoy liberty in a thousand years, or even in fifty, depends, I believe, in part on following Leonard's advice.

–Tom G. Palmer, January 2023

# INTRODUCTION: BUILDING THE LIBERTY MOVEMENT

By Brad Lips

"If Hayek was the architect of the modern liberty movement, Leonard Liggio was its builder."

These words were written by my predecessors as Atlas Network CEOs, John Blundell and Alex Chafuen, within a booklet of letters compiled on the occasion of Leonard's sixty-fifth birthday in 1998.

That booklet—and the companion birthday celebration that saw Leonard's admirers travel from all parts of the world to Charlottesville, Virginia—had a profound effect on me. I had been involved with Atlas Network for less than four months. I was only beginning to understand the role Atlas Network plays in promoting classical liberal ideas and bringing about free-market reforms. But I was awestruck by the gratitude that flowed toward this humble man, Leonard Liggio, then executive vice president of Atlas Network. He was not famous. He did not have power. But he was acknowledged by hundreds of people, from dozens of countries, for having meaningfully influenced the direction of their lives. He was a hero for quietly helping others explore great ideas in search of truths. Leonard's knowledge, wisdom, and gentle demeanor made him a trusted source of inspiration for generations of classical liberals.

Fifteen years later, as Leonard reached age eighty, Atlas Network joined with our friends at Liberty Fund and the Earhart Foundation, and with scores of individual donors, to launch

### Introduction: Building the Liberty Movement

the Leonard Liggio Lecture Series, which continues today as a central component of our largest annual event, Atlas Network's Liberty Forum, held in the United States each autumn.

We recently held the tenth Liggio Lecture. It's a good time to review what we have learned and how it relates to the task ahead: building a stronger liberty movement.

As expressed at the top, Leonard was a movement builder.

Attracting talented people to work in the same general direction, toward an appreciation of human dignity and free institutions, will always be a work in progress. I suspect Leonard would be proud of how the classical liberal community has grown and evolved in the years since his passing.

My flippant way of explaining a key change I've observed in recent years goes like this:

> Our community used to market itself as a Fan Club for Dead Economists, as though outsiders would be required to learn a secret handshake in order to be welcomed into our ranks. Today's freedom movement is more proactive in meeting bigger audiences where their interests are—reducing poverty, improving education, fostering innovation—and showing how we can achieve desirable outcomes by putting our classical liberal principles into action.

Leonard would have been excited about how these efforts are expanding our reach. After all, he was open-minded about where new fans of liberty would be found. He had friends among paleoconservatives and on the New Left. He was interested in how the world's great religions advance values that resonate with classical liberal principles. He was no partisan. He collaborated with equal enthusiasm with the conservatives at The Heritage Foundation and libertarians at The Cato Institute. That booklet

I mentioned, presented to Leonard for his sixty-fifth birthday, contained heartfelt tributes by thought leaders as diverse as Manuel Ayau, Gary Becker, Ed Crane, Ed Feulner, Israel Kirzner, Charles Koch, Vitali Naishul, Michael Novak, Andrea Rich, and Walter Williams. Surely, Leonard would want much more—not less—vigorous debate within our ranks.

But I suspect Leonard would have had a warning for us too.

In his presidential address to the Mont Pelerin Society in 2004 (see page 193) Leonard did not celebrate progress but issued warnings aimed at preventing classical liberalism from "calmly fad[ing] into the night." Specifically, he called attention to a dearth of impactful work coming from classical liberal academics:

> Many persons are doing fine work, which I appreciate. But few are making an impact. . . . Perhaps it is the problem of specialization. In order to achieve tenure and promotion, scholars must produce to the narrow demands of their departments. Their focus is aimed below the horizon. Lots of small pieces do not add up to widely read contributions. Similarly, such work must be non-controversial. Safety in the ordinary can mean work that stays below a higher radar screen.

Just as scholars may face perverse incentives inside the academy, those who labor with Atlas Network in think tanks and do-tanks also must navigate difficult tradeoffs. In an age of information abundance, policy institutes need to operate more like communications shops—with expertise in breaking through the clamor of a congested marketplace of ideas. The personnel best equipped to solve these critical challenges are rarely the people most studied in the nuances of the freedom philosophy.

This would make Leonard nervous.

## Introduction: Building the Liberty Movement

What's to prevent a more activist liberty movement from moving closer to narrative-advancing "clickbait" and away from a search for truth? To ensure Leonard's grand project will not wind up hollowed out, it is critical to energize new entrants to the freedom movement with a sincere love of ideas and with the norms and habits of truth-seeking.

This is why Leonard remained active until the end of his life with Liberty Fund, Philadelphia Society, Mont Pelerin Society, and Institute for Humane Studies. It's why he appreciated the volumes Tom Palmer edited for the growing ranks of Students for Liberty, and Linda Whetstone's work to get CD-ROMs of classical liberal texts into Arabic, Chinese, and other languages. It's why Leonard was proud of his honorary doctorate from Universidad Francisco Marroquín, and the prizes he was awarded by esteemed educational organizations like the Association for Private Enterprise Education, the Institute of Economic Studies Europe, and the Society for the Development of Austrian Economics.

This is also why our Liggio Lecture Program exists.

For the hundreds of first-timers at our Liberty Forum each year, we want the Liggio Lecture to put a spotlight on a thought-leader of rising influence. We want to feature a speaker who can stoke the curiosity of young people, so they discover a deeper love of free society principles, and so they come to appreciate why our movement is strongest

> **To ensure Leonard Liggio's grand project will not wind up hollowed out, it is critical to energize new entrants to the freedom movement with a sincere love of ideas and with the norms and habits of truth-seeking.**

when it's anchored in intellectual humility, free debate, and a sincere and energetic pursuit of truth.

I have titled this collection *Finding New Ideas in Old Ones*, as a reference to a "Liggiesque" phrase recollected by John Tomasi in his 2014 Liggio Lecture.

It's also a promise to readers: examining the lectures herein will spark your own curiosity and open new intellectual vistas for you to explore.

The first two chapters present the first two Liggio Lectures: one delivered by Jim Otteson with Leonard in attendance, and the aforementioned talk by John Tomasi, given shortly after Leonard's passing. These lectures draw lessons from the past to remind us that liberalism is fundamentally about the dignity of each human person. Its beauty comes from its universality, and its appeal comes from how—better than any competing philosophy—it promises opportunity, dignity, and uplift for society's most vulnerable members.

Chapters three through six provide tour-de-force ruminations on historical lessons that can inform thinking about four topics dear to Leonard's own studies: the U.S. Constitution, monetary theory, moral philosophy, and the modern regulatory state.

Randy Barnett lectures on the constitutional order that has been eroded, to the detriment of Americans' liberties, and that still could be restored. Larry White surveys seven centuries of monetary history to make the case for competition among and against government currencies. David Schmitz identifies a nineteenth-century wrong turn in moral philosophy that has bred incoherence in today's vocabulary around issues of justice and fairness. Judge Douglas

> **Examining the lectures herein will spark your own curiosity and open new intellectual vistas for you to explore.**

## Introduction: Building the Liberty Movement

Ginsburg brings a public choice perspective to the rise of the regulatory and administrative state in the United States over the twentieth century.

The next three chapters present ways forward for our movement that are incredibly relevant to the challenges of the 2020s. Peter Boettke looks at the temptations in the academy, affecting historians and economists, that will need to be resisted with intentionality to keep classical liberal scholarship robust. Lenore Ealy explores the challenge of winning new hearts and minds to classical liberalism, and proposes focusing less on politics and more on community to make the freedom philosophy actionable in people's lives. Gabriel Calzada's 2022 Liggio Lecture explores how governments eroded our liberties while claiming emergency powers during COVID and draws lessons from history to inform more appropriate responses to black swan events in the future.

A special Liggio Lecture was given in 2018 by Alex Chafuen, who used the occasion to offer personal reminiscences about Leonard, mostly drawn from the last two decades of Leonard's life, during which time they served together as colleagues at Atlas Network. To honor the spirit of Alex's talk, chapter 10 of this book includes photographs of Leonard, alongside accolades drawn from his friends and admirers.

This "personal touch" chapter reminds us that Leonard's intellectual contributions to the liberty movement are rivaled in importance by the personal example he set for the classical liberal community.

As we move further away from the date of Leonard's passing in October 2014, the Liggio Lecture Program will feature fewer people who had experience working directly with him.

May this volume help future leaders of the freedom movement to glimpse something of the character of the person we celebrate—humble, open, and kind.

May we find ourselves inspired to keep building our ranks with principled advocates of classical liberalism who operate with a similar generosity and spirit of inclusivity.

–Brad Lips, January 2023

# 1

# THE BEAUTY OF LIBERTY AND THE POWER OF SAYING NO

*By James Otteson*

---

The first Liggio Lecture was delivered at Atlas Network's 2013 Liberty Forum in New York City on November 14, 2013. It was the only one given during Leonard's lifetime or in his presence.

Jim Otteson, now the John T. Ryan Jr. Professor of Business Ethics at the University of Notre Dame, was then a professor of philosophy and economics at Yeshiva University in New York City. In his Liggio Lecture, he draws on his study of seventeenth-century English history to describe the beauty of liberty, rooted in the dignity of the individual, and to suggest a moral example for lovers of liberty to follow.

---

Ladies and gentlemen, it is a pleasure, and a humbling honor, to address you today.

Leonard Liggio is one of the giants in the history of liberty and a mentor and inspiration to me personally. When I was asked to give this inaugural Liggio Lecture, I confess I assumed there was some mistake. They must have meant to ask me for some ideas about who should give it. When it became clear that the invitation was meant for me, I was honored, but that quickly turned to despair. What on earth could I possibly say that would befit such a high, solemn occasion celebrating a figure like Leonard Liggio?

Racking my brain, I recalled a conversation I had with Leonard, about fifteen years ago. I was at the time a newly minted PhD in philosophy, and, of course, full of myself. I no longer recall where we were—a Liberty Fund conference? IHS?

Atlas Network? Earhart Foundation? (Leonard, of course, was, and is, everywhere)—but I do remember one part of our exchange. There were others present, and I had intended to make a remark that I hoped would impress everyone with my brilliance. So I sallied forth with the claim that the English Levellers of the 1600s (already I was impressing people, since I had even heard of these guys), who were sometimes identified as early progenitors of British classical liberalism, were in fact "basically socialists," which meant that perhaps socialism should be considered part of the British classical liberal tradition too! See how brilliant that was?

Leonard's response was simple and, as I came later to understand, typically Leonard: "No, you have that wrong." Apparently, I was so wrong that no elaboration was required.

Properly chastened and chagrined, I resolved to investigate. Who were these Levellers then? What did they agitate for? My investigation eventually led to my publishing in 2003 a five-volume edited collection of Leveller writings, many of which had been out of print and hardly accessible for centuries. That publication would not have happened were it not for Leonard's brief but potent remark. Thank you for that, Leonard.

So, who were the Levellers? Let me tell you about the greatest of them, John Lilburne. (Leonard, you will of course let us know if I get anything wrong.)

John Lilburne, or Free-Born John, as he was called, was born in Greenwich, England, in 1614 or 1615 to a family of low-level gentry, and he was an agitator and troublemaker almost from the beginning. In 1630 he began an apprenticeship to a Puritan cloth merchant in London, and shortly thereafter he joined the radical opposition to Charles I. In 1637, at the tender age of twenty-two, he smuggled from Holland outlawed copies of John Bastwick's account of the punishments he had suffered for denouncing Catholicism. When one of Lilburne's accomplices betrayed him to the archbishop's agents, Lilburne was arrested and tried before the ghastly Star Chamber, a body Lilburne detested and whose existence he protested. When Lilburne was brought to the bar before its judges, however, he refused to bow. He also refused to take the customary oath pledging to answer all interrogatories. Lilburne explained that as a free-born Englishman, he was, as he put it, the "peere and equall" of both the bishops and the Star Chamber's judges; there was therefore no reason for him to show the deference they demanded. For this shocking snub to the authority of the Chamber, he was fined, publicly whipped and pilloried, and finally imprisoned, receiving over time increasingly harsh punishment because he refused to stop denouncing the presumed authority of the bishops. Lilburne remained in prison until he was finally liberated by the Long Parliament in 1640 after a speech on his behalf by Cromwell (a man who himself would one day imprison Lilburne).

Thereafter, Lilburne became the most famous—or infamous—leader of the Levellers, a group of political agitators seeking extension of the franchise and other democratic rights. They were called "Levellers" not because they sought to level all property holdings—that was the position of a contemporaneous group called the Diggers (if I had had my history right, that's the group I would have mentioned in that fateful conversation with Leonard). The Levellers were called "Levellers" instead because they sought to equalize the privileges and rights of citizens: no one was by nature or by God entitled to less authority over his own life than anyone else, and no one was justified in asserting authority over anyone else without the latter's willing consent.

Lilburne was tireless and fearless. Even as he was put in the stocks, he issued one pamphlet and speech after another denouncing the presumed authority of the bishops, of the Star Chamber, of Parliament, and then even of Cromwell. He was again arrested, and he spent most of August 1645 to August 1647 in prison. But Lilburne was unbowed.

On May 1, 1649, while imprisoned yet again, he published a pamphlet arguing that people had a right to their private consciences by birth, not by pleasure of government; furthermore, the authority of each individual's conscience for himself was equal to that of everyone else; that therefore a person's religious beliefs were only his own business; and that therefore no one was entitled to any answers about others' beliefs.

Lilburne's message and example resonated. On May 2, 1649, some of the troops under Cromwell refused to follow Cromwell's orders to march on the Levellers. This defiance inspired mutiny of further troops, until by May 14 some twelve hundred men stopped taking orders from Cromwell, demanding instead the release of Lilburne. This was the last straw for Cromwell. Just after midnight on May 14, Cromwell and a contingent of men still loyal to him surprised and crushed what remained of the army sympathetic to the Levellers, effectively putting an end to the Levellers as an organized political movement.

Lilburne was then arrested and tried for treason. He defended himself and argued to the jury, in defiance of the explicit instructions of the judge, that as the judge's peers and equals, the members of the jury were empowered to judge not only the facts but also the law itself. To Cromwell's consternation, Lilburne was acquitted—and promptly returned to denouncing Cromwell's increasing imperiousness. Cromwell was so infuriated that in 1653 he re-arrested Lilburne and had him tried for treason again. Again Lilburne defended himself, and again he was acquitted. This second acquittal even led to a large popular demonstration in support of Lilburne, symbolized by thousands of sympathizers wearing the Levellers' characteristic sea-green ribbons on hats and clothing. This sufficiently worried Cromwell that he decided to keep Lilburne in prison despite the acquittals. Lilburne remained in prison until 1655, when he converted to the Quaker faith and apparently, finally, foreswore his aggressive, confrontational ways. In 1657, with his health failing, he was granted parole to visit his wife, Elizabeth. Exhausted from years of imprisonment and torture in his fight for liberty, he died in her arms at the age of forty-three.

Lilburne was no philosopher, but his agitations formed a surprisingly coherent philosophy of individualism, from which he derived several specific political policies. These included the rights to be free of arbitrary seizures, to a trial by jury, and to face one's accusers in open court. He also called for the extension of the franchise to all the freeborn men of England; he advocated free trade and private property; and he called for an abolition of legal economic privileges like state-enforced monopolies. He denounced the Levant Company's chartered monopoly of trade with the Middle East, arguing that the right to trade with whomever one wished was one of mankind's natural rights. Thus Lilburne was one of the earliest advocates of what would come to be recognized as classical liberalism, defending private property some fifty years before John Locke, and free markets almost 150 years before Adam Smith.

When Lilburne had been brought before the Star Chamber in 1637, he had stood his ground, asserting his equal right as an individual to the freedoms anyone else enjoyed. In 1641, Lilburne saw the Star Chamber abolished. That, ladies and gentlemen, was a great moral leap forward, elevating the individual—even

> **That was a great moral leap forward, elevating the individual—even the low, the mean, the disrespected individuals—to the status of a moral agent equal in dignity to those in the favored classes.**

the low, the mean, the disrespected individuals—to the status of a moral agent equal in dignity to those in the favored classes.

This conception of morality and human personhood spread and eventually gave rise to many of the institutions we today in the West often take for granted. If no one, regardless of class, family, or wealth, had any justified authority over anyone else, then individuals no longer need to beg leave from their "superiors" to own property, to select lines of work, to trade or exchange or cooperate with others, to worship and associate as they judge fit. Each person's success or failure in life was fundamentally his own responsibility, even if, of course, it necessarily involved relying on willing others. Individuality, diversity, and, of course, various inequalities—except formal or legal inequality—arose, and with it the unprecedented growth in human accomplishment, in material prosperity, in longevity and health and nutrition that we have seen occur in the world in the last two centuries.

Now, of course, Lilburne wasn't solely responsible for this, but he inspired many others and was emblematic of a changing conception of morality and thus politics. The lesson to draw from the example of Lilburne is that each individual is unique and precious, and that fact issues a moral imperative of equal respect. The classical liberal government that promotes justice for all while at the same time respecting each person's unique individual dignity as an equal moral agent is consistent with, even an embodiment of, this moral imperative.

I believe this conception of human moral agency is a shining example of the beauty—both the moral and the aesthetic beauty—of liberty. The inspiring example of Free-Born John drives the point home. And there are many other examples one might adduce.

The contrasting position, however, is dramatically illustrated by Rainer Maria Rilke's poem, "The Panther," which tells of a powerful and beautiful panther that, once free, now sees the world from behind bars, indeed behind "a thousand bars." As Rilke tells us, the great cat's beauty and power rapidly decline—not because he grows older, but because his spirit is caged and thus defeated. Sooner than one could expect, the panther is, though alive, truly dead, because behind the bars he is no longer really a panther.

Now the panther's well-intended zoo keepers will say that in the wild his life is full of dangers. Nature can be parsimonious and unforgiving, whereas the zoo keepers are benevolent and protective. So although behind the bars the panther is not free, he is at least safe and comfortable. They have a point. But the pampered and protected panther is still a caged panther—and so not really a panther at all.

Still, since the panther is not a full moral agent, perhaps you're not inclined to value its freedom very highly, and so you're inclined to think that a zoo-keeper morality is acceptable in this case. Fair enough. Human beings, however, are moral agents, and so the zoo-keeper morality is unacceptable for them. Living free is uncertain and sometimes dangerous, and it does involve both success and failure. But both one's successes and one's failures are one's own. They belong to you and to me, and it is the true dignity of humanity to fully exercise all its abilities in striving and contending. As Calvin Coolidge, one of our greatest—if most unappreciated—presidents, said:

> Unless [. . .] people struggle to help themselves, no one else will or can help them. It is out of such struggle that there comes the strongest evidence of their true independence and nobility, and there is struck off a rough and incomplete economic justice, and there develops a strong and rugged [. . .] character. It represents a spirit for which there could be no substitute. It justifies the claim that they are worthy to be free. ("The Price of Freedom," 1923)

Human beings, I contend, are capable of becoming worthy to be free. Human beings become noble, and (I contend) beautiful, by the vigorous use of their faculties, and they become dignified when their lives are their own, when all the forced care and protection of others is taken away, and the bars are thrown open.

Returning now to Lilburne and liberty. We tend to think that at the heart of liberty lies the ability to do what one wants. Of course that's limited by the similar freedom of others, but the idea is that liberty is about having the power to say "yes." I suggest, however, that it is in fact the power of saying no that most powerfully exemplifies our moral agency. And it is when we, like Free-Born John, refuse to bow that we assume our place as free, equal, and beautiful moral agents.

Indeed, human liberty has historically developed not gradually but by great leaps—and in each of the great cases, it has been by some people, often at first just one person, saying "no." No, I will not compromise what I believe. No, I will not acknowledge your authority over me. No, I will not accept your interpretation of my duty to God. No, you do not rule me. No, I am not your property. No, I am not less than human. No, your moral agency is not inherently superior to mine. No, I will not work for you. No, I will not pay your tributes. No, I will not marry you. No, I do not accept your judgment of how I live my life. No, I will not be quiet. No, I will not let you invade my privacy. No, I am not a second-class citizen.

On the opposite side of this is the shameful, and ugly, fact that most of human history has been characterized by our relentless attempts to control one another. My God are we meddling busybodies! Cast your mind's eye back over human history: how much of it is marked by the ugliness of one group of people trying to mind, control, repress, redirect, manage, reform, reeducate, restrain, command, rule, dominate, bully, browbeat, humiliate, superintend, engineer, organize, supervise, govern, or nudge others? Yet almost all of the great and shining moments of human history are when someone stands up and says: "No! You may have the power to coerce me, but I do not recognize your moral authority to do so."

Today, our self-anointed superiors often justify their interposition in our lives on the grounds that they know what choices we should make to make our lives better. The latter-day Puritans and Inquisitors say: Don't worry, we are here to help you. If we know that smoking and eating doughnuts and drinking twenty-ounce sodas and driving motorcycles and starting taxi companies and serving the homeless your homemade food and braiding hair without a license and using an incandescent light bulb and not recycling [and on and endlessly on] are all bad, it would be wrong not to intervene—right?

> **Human liberty has historically developed not gradually but by great leaps—and in each of the great cases, it has been by some people, often at first just one person, saying "no."**

Wrong! On the contrary, it is precisely this paternalistic meddling that shows others a profound, and immoral, disrespect. For that says: "We do not believe you are competent to lead your life properly, so we shall undertake to do it for you." That may be appropriate for children or for the mentally infirm, but it is an unacceptable imposition on the equal moral agency of adults. Ladies and gentlemen, I submit to you that having a person in government serving as a "Regulation Czar" is an affront to everything the long and proud and beautiful history of liberty stands for. It is to our shame that we tolerate it.

To our actual and would-be czars, then, I say: Not even God believed He should restrict mankind's ability to choose only the right: when He created man, God gave him free choice, which necessarily entailed the ability to choose the wrong. Well, if it was good enough for God, it is good enough for you, Cass Sunstein. That doesn't mean you can never help another, but it does mean that you must respect others' agency when you undertake to do so. If they decide not to do what you want them to do, if they resist your impositions and your nudges, if they behave in the gloriously unpredictable way free people do, you must respect them. They have the right to say no to you. And, as we should all know by now, no means no.

Let me now come to my conclusion. What Leonard Liggio did for me those many years ago is something he has done for countless others over the years. He has not only argued for, but his life has actually exemplified, the principles I have described. In inspiring me to rethink my positions on my own, he respected my moral agency even as he reminded me that intellectual laziness serves no one—including me. Liberty is too important not to get the story right and for me not to figure out how I might personally contribute, in however small a way, to its unfolding moral arc.

What, then, would be the best way not only to thank Leonard but to honor him and his legacy?

By doing the same yourself.

I exhort you, then, each of you, to look at the opportunities available to you, and to seek out ways that you too might contribute, in your own unique but indispensable way, to the protection, preservation, and extension of the moral beauty of liberty. Perhaps this will entail exercising your own power of saying "no." Perhaps like me you too will decide to prosecute your own campaign of what I call Guerilla Liberty™—entrepreneurially and opportunistically finding your own ways to deny, and even subvert, the assumed authority of those who presume to superintend you. I won't tell you more about my own Guerilla

Liberty campaign, not only because the NSA is listening right now (though they are) but also because I believe in the power of decentralized spontaneous order and division of labor. So I cannot know how you should expend your efforts; maybe you yourself don't know—yet. But I do know that your time on this earth is absolutely limited, and the threats to liberty are real—and advancing. So get started, right now, and put every remaining minute you have on this earth to good use. Like all beautiful things, liberty is fragile, and a free society is rare indeed; they require continuous maintenance by those who appreciate their blessings. When they are threatened, however—as they are now—they require all hands on deck. That means me; that means you.

Now, we may not be successful. And as many in this room can personally attest, fighting for liberty carries risks. But moral duty requires us to fight nonetheless.

Ladies and gentlemen, there is a lot of ugliness in this world, and there is nothing uglier than coercion and paternalism. My call, then, is really to minimize ugliness and promote beauty: moral and aesthetic beauty.

There are a lot of beautiful people in this room, starting with Leonard Liggio. What we stand to gain, then, not only for ourselves but for all other equal moral agents, including the future souls on whom peaceful and prosperous civilization will depend, is the priceless gift that people like Leonard and John Lilburne and so many others have spent their lives nurturing and protecting: the exquisitely beautiful and precious treasure of freedom.

> **Like all beautiful things, liberty is fragile, and a free society is rare indeed; they require continuous maintenance by those who appreciate their blessings.**

# 2

# MARKET SOCIETY: THE TINY TIM DEFENSE

By John Tomasi

---

The second Liggio Lecture was delivered at Atlas Network's 2014 Liberty Forum in New York City on November 13, 2014. Leonard had died the previous month, and his friend John Blundell—another beloved figure in the history of Atlas Network—had passed away in July. Early in his lecture, John Tomasi references the photo of the two of them that we have included on page 30, taken by Greg Lindsay (founder of Centre for Independent Studies, Australia) at an Institute for Humane Studies seminar in 1981. We also use italicized parentheticals to note two sets of slides used in the talk.

In his Liggio Lecture, John Tomasi argues that a foundational premise of the social justice movement, in fact, presents an opportunity to make a strong case for free markets and individual liberty. John was then the Romeo Elton Professor of Natural Philosophy at Brown University. He now serves as president of Heterodox Academy.

---

Good afternoon. I am deeply honored to be giving the Liggio Lecture this year. I first met Leonard in the summer of 1988 at an Institute for Humane Studies weeklong "Liberty in Society" seminar. That seminar was taught by a remarkable group of liberty people: Leonard, Walter Grinder, Ralph Raico, Randy Barnett, and this really dynamic young guy named Tom Palmer.

The format in those days—and, I think, still—is that there are lectures all day long and then in the evening, over beer, we talk about ideas. And one evening, I remember I was sitting with Tom Palmer in a small group, and Tom said to us,

### Market Society: The Tiny Tim Defense

"You're the next generation for liberty! You're going to be the leaders. You're going to come up with ideas we've never even thought of."

I was so excited to be hearing that, as a young person, and the next day I sat at lunch with Leonard, and I told him what Tom had said, and maybe it's true, and it's so exciting, and I babbled on and on. And Leonard sort of sat there, in his quiet way, just taking it all in. And I finally stopped my babbling. He looked at me, gave me a smile, with a sly little look in his eye—(*pointing at Leonard, to the left of John Blundell in the 1981 photo below*) exactly that smile, and that twinkle in his eye. And then he said to me: "John, the best place to find new ideas is in the old ones."

So what I'm going to do today, in honor of that Liggiesque thought, is share with you a new idea. It's an idea that some of you, I expect, may initially resist—and maybe resist even after I finish. I don't know. But I'm going to present it, in the spirit of Leonard, by looking into some old ideas.

So let's take a little journey back first, to 1909, in London. That year, there was an incredibly popular play called *A Message from the Forties*. The title was a reference to the 1840s, when the Corn Laws were still in effect. People were entering factory work now for the first time. The Corn Laws had the effect

> **And then he said to me: 'John, the best place to find new ideas is in the old ones.'**

of inflating the profits of the aristocratic landholders but also raising the price of bread and therefore making it really tough for factory workers to feed their children. This play, *A Message from the Forties*, was a spoof on Dickens's *A Christmas Carol*. The part of Scrooge was not played by some evil capitalist; rather, Scrooge was played by a person who was against free trade and for tariffs. And Bob Cratchit was played by a factory worker from Manchester who was very concerned about getting bread for his children—most of all, Tiny Tim.

In the course of the play, Scrooge is eventually reformed. The climax of the play is when he is visited by the ghost of Richard Cobden, who reminds him: "Care about the poor; think of the children; abandon this opposition to free trade."

That idea, that free trade is for the poor, was common—a common idea in the free-trade days of England.

*(John shows political cartoons as described in the paragraphs that follow)*

You can see the children in these cartoons are the ones who are being threatened by the taxes. That free markets are for the poor was a common theme.

The free-trade cupboard has a big loaf of bread, but the evil tariff reformers who are opposed to free trade are trying to raid the free-trade cupboard. And, again, it's the children and the women, it's the weak, whom we're supposed to think about most

## Market Society: The Tiny Tim Defense

of all when we think of whose lives are improved by the benefits of free trade.

That idea is rooted in works such as that of Adam Smith, who was famously concerned for the poor. This is one of my favorite lines from his *The Wealth of Nations*.

> That state is properly opulent in which opulence is easily come at, or in which a little labour, properly and judiciously employed, is capable of procuring any man a great abundance of all the necessaries and conveniences of life. . . . National opulence is the opulence of the whole people.

The idea is that—in a decent country, in a just society or a good society, a prosperous society—things should be arranged so that anyone who is willing to work can do well. Anyone who is willing to put their time in, to make a real effort, should be able to succeed. And, as Smith puts it, "National opulence is the opulence of the whole people."

Now, something happened along the way, because the party of free markets is no longer the party of the poor. And what happened, I think, was this term arose: "social justice."

People who became advocates of social justice were people who thought that you had to pursue social justice by way of big state institutions. And so the term "social justice"—which could have been, and should have been, attached conceptually to the idea of helping the poor—became attached in popular language to the idea of big government.

For that reason, people on the free-market side came to think of the term "social justice" as meaning something like a call for big government. Thus, they rejected it. That idea became fixed in philosophical terms in the cement of philosophy in the 1970s, thanks to a very important book in 1971 by John Rawls called *A*

*Theory of Justice*, which is the seminal statement of what social justice is. And then a few years later, Friedrich Hayek wrote *The Mirage of Social Justice*, in which Hayek raises some concerns, perhaps, about social justice. Certainly, his refrain throughout the book is essentially, "I hate social justice."

Why does he say that? Here's a quick summary of Hayek's view:

Hayek believes that we should think of a free society—a society in which people connect and grow and live together—as being a cosmos, or a spontaneous order, or an emergent order. In a free society, people move around individually or in groups; they connect with one another; and they change the world in unpredictable ways. The output is something that grows rather than something that's made. It's a product of human action, not of any human design.

> **For Hayek, there is a basic principle: only products of deliberate human design can be called just or unjust.**

Like the specific pattern of crystals on a collection of rock candy, the specific pattern of distribution of goods and society at any given moment is not something that anyone could have foreseen. It just emerges that way. And for Hayek, there is a basic principle: only products of deliberate human design can be called just or unjust. Therefore, if "social justice" now becomes a corrective to the distribution of goods, the only way we can make sense of that term applied to our society is by changing the nature of our society itself. We have to transform this natural, grown thing—the free society—into an organized, planned society.

*(John transitions from a slide showing rock candy crystals to a built-with-Legos simulation of the Death Star from* Star Wars.*)*

## Market Society: The Tiny Tim Defense

Yes, I always choose my examples to make my case.... So, we can only get social justice if we change our society from sugar rock candy to Death Stars.

That's the story, right? That's the story I was told in grad school. That's the story kids are still being told in grad school. But it's actually a *weird* story because, interestingly, it's not true even historically. I recently came across some letters that Pete Boettke, a professor at George Mason University, had sent to me—a correspondence between two great defenders of liberty, Friedrich Hayek and Jim Buchanan, both Nobel Prize winners. In Hayek's letter, written in November 1965, he says something shocking. He basically wrote: "Hey, Jim, you know, I saw your recent article on ethics; that was really great. You know, I'm really thinking about this question: What are the foundations for the free society?'" And then he writes, "The only modern philosopher from whom I've received some help for this is John Rawls of MIT." Rawls was a first-year assistant professor at MIT. He had just one published article at the time.

Three weeks later, Buchanan replied, "Yeah, I think Rawls is . . ." Well, this is how I paraphrase it: "I think Rawls is the balls, too. And I hope that his ideas can have some impact." As an aside: notice that it's very common for academics, when we want to wind down, we often read our own books. It's very common. But here we have Hayek and Buchanan, the great defenders of the free society, complimenting John Rawls from the other side. What's that about?

It gets even weirder. In the book *The Mirage of Social Justice,* in which Hayek basically makes a belief in social justice sound as ludicrous as a belief in witches, there's something shocking in the preface, page 13. He says, "Oh, by the way, as I'm finishing this book, I happened to have read this book by John Rawls. Actually, I studied it pretty carefully. It seems to me that despite

John Tomasi

what you all think, the differences between my view and that of Professor Rawls is more verbal than substantive."

What?! The great critic of social justice has a note in the preface saying he affirms Rawls's view? How can this be? There's weirder stuff, too. It'll come in a minute.

So what's going on? What is the idea that Hayek and Buchanan find so attractive in Rawls? Rawls's first article was this crazy technical piece, but it provided the foundation for the growth of Rawls's view. It was the foundation for his view that never changed for his entire career.

So, in that early article, which Hayek is going to quote, Rawls is asking this weird philosopher's question: What is justice a property of? The kind of question philosophers ask a lot. I know it sounds like it makes no sense at all, but it is this: If you have a theory, a device of representation that can produce a measuring stick of social justice, what is it that that thing should measure? What should it be applied to? As one answer, Rawls says, social justice could be a property of particular distributions—that is, who's got what in society at any given moment. That's the way social justice is often used in popular discourse. But Rawls says that that way of thinking about justice makes no sense. In fact, if that's the standard social justice is meant to apply to—the particular holdings at any given moment—then there's no solution to the question "What counts as social justice?" It's insoluble, because people keep moving and changing and doing things.

So instead, Rawls said—this is his first big move in his academic career—justice is not a property of holdings (the wealth barometer); rather, justice is a property of institutions. So if you want to know if society is just or unjust, by some theory of social justice, we don't look at the holdings that people have, we look instead to the institutions. And we look in particular, Rawls says, to the long-run institutions for the great classes of mankind, we could say. How well does the set of institutions do, say, for the least-well-off working class over the course of a generation or two compared to other possible systems? And, as I mentioned here, Hayek buried in the back of the book that quote of the technical piece of Rawls. And again, that shows me that when he and Buchanan were saying, "This guy Jack Rawls, he's okay," what they were saying was, "This is big." Because the popular uses of "social justice," that require the big government, all are using it in the other way. They're using "social justice" to refer to particular distributions that might be corrected by the big government. But the philosophical account says that that's incoherent. Rawls's account says that. Their guy says that. Rather, it's institutions which need to be judged from a general point of view.

It opens up a rather interesting possibility of thinking about spontaneous order, because remember that old sugar candy on the stick versus the Death Star? And you recall Hayek's basic moral standard that only products of human design can properly be described as just or unjust. Well, if you think about where rock candy comes from, then we notice that it looks like it's a design. It's a design for liberty. It's a design of a certain constitutional structure, let's say, that will allow and support spontaneous processes to emerge. We can therefore judge the justice of spontaneous orders not by examining who's got a big crystal or who's got a small crystal—rather, we evaluate this principle of design, this set of institutions, by asking, "How well do people fare in a free society? How well do people fare—let's say the lowest-paid working class, the ones that Smith was caring about—how well do they fare in a pro-market society as opposed to an alternative society such as socialist ones when we let things run over the course of a generation or two?"

So we ask the question by the most sophisticated, technical philosopher's position from the left—we ask the question of social justice in those terms. And I think when you ask the question in those terms, and think about Adam Smith, and think about those pictures I showed you earlier about the free-trade movement in England being based on the idea that trade is good for the poor and for the weak, we suddenly see that there's no reason for people who care about free markets, and are committed to individual liberty and personal responsibility, there's no reason for us to be afraid of the term "social justice." Quite the contrary.

> **There's no reason for people who care about free markets, and are committed to individual liberty and personal responsibility, to be afraid of the term 'social justice.' Quite the contrary.**

If the test for a just society is which set of social institutions over time—over a generation or two—does the best for the least-well-off working class (that's Rawls's test), then we have nothing to fear at all. We can match up our best institutions, our preferred institutional forms, against their preferred institutional forms. And when you do that, I think you find that the free market wins.

So, the idea that I want to leave you with—you probably already see it—is that we, maybe all of us in this room, are the party of social justice.

3

# RESTORING OUR REPUBLICAN CONSTITUTION

By Randy E. Barnett

---

The third Liggio Lecture was delivered at Atlas Network's 2015 Liberty Forum in New York City on November 12, 2015.

Randy Barnett serves as the Patrick Hotung Professor of Constitutional Law at Georgetown University where he directs the Georgetown Center for the Constitution. He used his Liggio Lecture to preview his book, *Our Republican Constitution: Securing the Liberty and Sovereignty of We the People*. In his book and this lecture, he identifies the divide between those who view the founding document as fundamentally majoritarian or "democratic," and those who view it as "republican," which means it is protective of fundamental rights and individual sovereignty.

---

Thank you, Tom, for that wonderful introduction. It's a pleasure to be here. It's such a great honor to be giving the Leonard Liggio lecture. I first met Leonard when I was a first-year law student in first semester of first-year law in 1974, when I came down to New York to hear him give a lecture at Fordham, and in the audience was Murray Rothbard. So that day, the day I met Leonard was the day I met Murray. And then just one thing led to another after that. You can imagine those two guys together.

Leonard has done so much for my career. I'm sure I wouldn't be here today if it weren't for him. But I also know him well enough to know that he would not want me talking about him so much. I was also greatly pleased to be here for the first Liggio Lecture when Leonard himself was here and could attend this lecture.

But I will now move off of Leonard, which he would want me to do if he were here, and get on to my talk, because Leonard was all about the ideas and not at all about personality.

And the talk that I'm going to give you is a preview of my next book, *Our Republican Constitution*, which will be published by HarperCollins in April of next year. It's going to be my first trade book that's been written for a popular audience. So let me just start here. In 1789, James Madison had a problem, after living for ten years under the Articles of Confederation, Madison had worked tirelessly behind the scenes to bring about a convention to devise a new constitution. In September of 1786, he participated in a preliminary convention in Annapolis, Maryland. By 1787, he had secured enough support of such key players as George Washington and Ben Franklin to convene a Constitutional Convention in Philadelphia.

But now the pressure was on the thirty-six-year-old Madison. Before journeying to Philadelphia, he crammed for the gathering like a student for his exams, from a chest of books that he'd been given by his friend and mentor, Thomas Jefferson. For the cerebral Madison had a truly fundamental problem to solve. Like many others, he had concluded that the American regime governed by the Articles of Confederation was grossly inadequate and contrary to what the Virginia Declaration of Rights had called "the common benefit, protection, and security of the people." But why was this happening? Why had the republicanism of the Founding Generation failed them so?

For the previous thirteen years, the people of the United States had been governed by thirteen separate entities; state governments under the Articles of Confederation were thought to be republican. The Founders had thrown off rule by an aristocratic few in favor of rule by a democratic many. If under aristocracy, the many are screwed by the few, the democratic or republican alternative was premised on the belief that the people wouldn't screw themselves. This is a technical-legal phraseology. This is probably some kind of a residual effect of having been a Cook County State's Attorney before I became a law professor.

But anyway, the theory was the people wouldn't screw themselves, but this republican theory had unexpectedly proven to be false. State legislators began enacting debtor relief laws that both undermined the rights of creditors and impaired economic prosperity, which requires a credit market that can safely rely on the obligations of private contracts to collect from debtors. States also erected a debilitating assortment of trade barriers to protect their own businesses from competing firms in neighboring states. There was, as a result of all this, a national economic downturn.

So republican government, as it was then conceived, was clearly not working for the common benefit, protection, and security of the people. But why not? To answer this question, in April of 1787, largely for his own benefit, Madison composed an essay called "The Vices of the Political System of the United States." In "Vices," Madison identified the source of the problem in what he called "the injustice of the laws of the states."

The causes of this evil—he referred to it as "this evil"—he contended, could be traced to "the representative bodies in the states and ultimately to the people themselves." This, he wrote, called, "into question, the fundamental principle of republican government, that the majority who rule in such governments are the safest guardians of both the public good and private rights." That was the central premise he said was called into question.

Madison concluded that we must be far more realistic about popular majorities. All civilized societies, he explains, "are divided into different interests and factions as they may happen to be creditors or debtors, rich or poor, husbandmen, merchants or manufacturers, members of different religious sects, followers of different political leaders, inhabitants of different districts, owners of different kinds of property, et cetera." In a democracy, the debtors outnumber the creditors and the poor outnumber the rich. The larger group can simply outvote the smaller. The majority, however composed, Madison continued, "ultimately give the law."

Whenever therefore an apparent interest or common passion unites a majority, what is to restrain them from unjust violations of the rights and interests of the minority or of individuals? To illustrate the problem, Madison posed the following thought experiment: "Place three individuals in a situation where the interest of each depends on the voice of the others and give to two of them an interest opposed to the rights of the third. Will the latter be secure? The prudence of every man," he said "would shun the danger."

Likewise, "Will 2,000 in a like situation, be less likely to encroach the rights of the 1,000?" In short, under the democratic vision of republicanism, there is nothing stopping a majority of the polity from engaging in self-dealing at the expense of the minority. Madison concluded that what was needed was nothing less than a new republican form of government that would address the weaknesses of democratic state governments while preserving popular sovereignty. As Madison put it, "To secure the public good in private rights against the danger of such a faction, and at the same time to preserve the spirit in form of popular government is the great object in which our inquiries are directed."

Now, Madison was not alone in locating the ills facing the nation in the majoritarian democracy of the states. At the Philadelphia Convention, Edmund Randolph, who became our first attorney general of the United States under George Washington observed that "the general object was to provide a cure for the evils under which the U.S. labored, and that in tracing these evils to their origin, every man found it in the turbulence and follies of democracy." Elbridge Gerry from Massachusetts stated, "The evils we experienced flow from an excess of democracy."

Roger Sherman of Connecticut contended that the people "immediately should have as little to do as may be about the government." Gouverneur Morris from Pennsylvania noted that "every man of observation has seen in the democratic branches of state legislatures, precipitation—in Congress, changeableness—and in every department, excesses against personal liberty, private property, and personal safety." Now, even those who remain more amenable to democracy like George Mason of Virginia admitted that "we have been too democratic in forming state governments."

At the conclusion of the convention, anxious citizens gathered around Independence Hall to learn what had been produced behind closed doors. It is said that as Benjamin Franklin left the building, a woman in the crowd asked him, "Well, doctor, what have we got? A republic or a monarchy?" Franklin is said to have responded, "A republic, if you can keep it." While the new form of government devised in Philadelphia was not a monarchy, neither was it democratic. Yet Franklin still called it a republic. This was because the meaning of that term had just been changed by the men in the building from which Franklin was leaving.

> **'Well, doctor, what have we got? A republic or a monarchy?' Franklin is said to have responded, 'A republic, if you can keep it.'**

A republican constitution was no longer a democratic one, if it ever had been. In my book, *Our Republican Constitution*, I contend that these two fundamentally divergent views of the Constitution divide us even today. I call these divergent conceptions the "Democratic Constitution" and the "Republican Constitution," but I don't intend these labels to be partisan. There are political conservatives who hew to some aspects of the Democratic Constitution and some progressives who adopt aspects of the Republican one. Many people flit between conceptions depending on which happens to conform to the results they like. I chose the terms Democratic and Republican Constitutions because both terms have deep roots in our constitutional history, and neither is pejorative. I dislike arguments by labels and both these labels have a positive connotation.

## The Democratic Constitution

At its core, this debate is about the meaning of popular sovereignty. Those who adhere to the Democratic Constitution hold a different conception of popular sovereignty than those who adhere to the Republican Constitution. So let me begin by explaining the role that popular sovereignty plays in our thinking about the Constitution.

The concept of popular sovereignty was first developed in the United States at the time of our founding. Back then it was a first principle of political theory that sovereignty—or the right to rule—must reside somewhere in any polity. While the ultimate sovereign was thought to be God who ruled the world, on earth, monarchs claimed to be the sovereign rulers of their own people, ruling by delegation from God, or what was called divine right.

When the Americans had their revolution and rejected the rule of the English King, political theory required them to say who was sovereign in their new polity. The answer they gave was that "the people" themselves were the ultimate sovereign. But this raised at least as many questions as it solved. If "sovereignty" were an answer to the question of who has the right to rule, in what sense do the people rule? This seems like a contradiction. We need government to rule the people, and yet the people themselves are supposed to be the ultimate ruler?

What I am calling the Democratic Constitution is one way to address the problem of how the sovereign people can be said to rule. If sovereignty is conceived as residing in the people collectively or as a body, then popular sovereignty means rule by the people as a body—and "rule by the people" means rule *according to the will of the people*—where "will" is a fancy word for "desire."

Of course, it makes perfect sense to talk about the will or desire of a sovereign monarch. But in what sense does a body of individual persons have a collective will or desire? What is the will or desire of the group in this room at the moment?

No one who makes assertions about "the will of the people" ever claims that there must be, or ever is, a unanimous consensus of everyone to some particular desire. In practice, the collective "will of the people" must rest on the desires of a majority or super-majority of the people. It does not—because it cannot—rest on the desires of everyone. Therefore, in operation, a conception of popular sovereignty based on rule according to the will of the people means rule according to the will of a majority of the people.

So the Democratic Constitution starts with a collective vision of popular sovereignty based on the will of the people as a group, and the ultimate will of the people can only be that of the majority or greater number.

According to this conception, then, a legitimate constitution is a Democratic Constitution. It sets up institutional mechanisms by which the desires of a majority of the people can be expressed. This is known as "representative democracy."

If a well-constructed Democratic Constitution, based on a collective conception of popular sovereignty, is one that allows the views of the majority to prevail, then a number of important implications follow.

First and foremost, any principle or practice that gets in the way of the will of the majority or majority rule is presumptively illegitimate and requires special justification.

Under the Democratic Constitution, the only individual rights that are legally enforceable are a product of majoritarian will—whether the will of majorities in the legislature who create *legal* rights, or the will of majorities who ratified the Constitution who created *constitutional* rights.

So, under the Democratic Constitution, *first comes government*, and *then come rights*. First one needs to establish a polity with a legislature that represents the will of the people, and this legislature will then decide which rights get legal protection and which do not.

The Democratic Constitution is a "living constitution" whose meaning evolves to align with contemporary popular desires, so that today's majority is not bound by what is called "the dead hand of the past." After all, by what right does the will or desires of yesterday's majority override the will of the majority today?

Under the Democratic Constitution, unelected judges who are not accountable to the majority present what Alexander Bickel called the "counter-majoritarian difficulty." Judges are not selected to represent the desires of anyone. They are appointed, not elected, and in the federal system they serve for life. To the extent they invalidate popularly enacted laws, these unelected and unaccountable judges are thwarting the will of the people as manifested in their elected representatives.

Under the Democratic Constitution, judges are told they should exercise their power of judicial review with "restraint." They should defer to the will of the popularly elected branches by adopting a "presumption of constitutionality" that simply presumes—perhaps irrebuttably— that properly elected legislatures have acted properly when they restrict the liberties of the people.

Randy E. Barnett

For the people are only restricting themselves—we are told—and how they wish to govern themselves is for their democratically selected representatives to decide.

Today, the belief in the Democratic Constitution is so pervasive among both progressives and conservatives—and among Democrats and Republicans—that you might be sitting there wondering what other view of the Constitution there could be. Perhaps the most important purpose of this talk is simply to identify and describe this other view—what I am calling the Republican Constitution—so that you can recognize it as a distinct vision of the Constitution.

### The Republican Constitution

What separates the Republican Constitution from the Democratic Constitution is its conception of "popular sovereignty." Where the Democratic Constitution views sovereignty as residing in the people *collectively* or as a group, the Republican Constitution views sovereignty as residing in the people *as individuals*.

A Republican Constitution views the natural and inalienable rights of these joint and equal sovereign individuals as preceding the formation of governments, so "first come rights and then comes government." Indeed, as I noted yesterday, the Declaration of Independence tells us, it is *"to secure these rights,"* that "Governments are instituted among Men."

This individualist conception of popular sovereignty was most

> **Where the Democratic Constitution views sovereignty as residing in the people *collectively* or as a group, the Republican Constitution views sovereignty as residing in the people *as individuals*.**

strikingly presented in the first great constitutional case decided by the Supreme Court in 1793, just four years after the Constitution was adopted. The case was *Chisholm v. Georgia*, and it involved a lawsuit brought against the state of Georgia by a citizen of South Carolina. The suit was for breach of contract to pay for goods that had been supplied to Georgia during the Revolutionary War.

Article III, Section 2 of the Constitution specifies that "[t]he judicial power of the United States shall extend to . . . controversies, *between a state and citizens of another State,*" which certainly seems to cover a suit brought by a citizen of South Carolina against the state of Georgia. The state of Georgia, however, asserted that it had sovereign immunity from such a suit, and refused even to appear in the Supreme Court to defend itself.

In *Chisholm,* the Supreme Court, by a vote of four to one, rejected Georgia's assertion of sovereign immunity. The majority concluded instead that members of the public could sue state governments because "sovereignty" rests with the people rather than with the states. The justices in *Chisholm* affirmed that, in America, the states are not kings, and their legislatures are not the supreme successors to the Crown.

Justice James Wilson—who had been among the most influential of delegates to the constitutional convention—began his opinion by stressing that the Constitution nowhere uses the term "sovereignty." "To the Constitution of the United States the term Sovereign, is totally unknown," he wrote. There was only one place in the Constitution "where it could have been used with propriety," he observed, referring to the Preamble. "But, even in that place it would not, perhaps, have comported with the delicacy of those, who ordained and established that Constitution. They might have announced themselves 'Sovereign' people of the United States: But serenely conscious of the fact, they avoided the ostentatious declaration."

Wilson contended that, if the term sovereign is to be used at all, it should refer to the individual person. "[L]aws derived from the pure source of equality and justice must be founded on the CONSENT of those whose obedience they require. The sovereign, when traced to this source, must be found in *the man*." In other words, obedience must rest on the consent of the individual person who is asked to obey the law. Wilson believed that the only reason "a free man is bound by human laws, is, that he binds himself."

For Wilson, states were nothing more than an aggregate of free individuals. "If one free man, an original sovereign," may bind himself to the jurisdiction of the court, "why may not an aggregate of free men, a collection of original sovereigns, do this likewise? If the dignity of each singly is undiminished; the dignity of all jointly must be unimpaired."

Justice Wilson was not alone in locating sovereignty in the individual person. In his opinion in *Chisholm*, Chief Justice John Jay—who, with Madison and Hamilton, had authored some of the early Federalist Papers—referred tellingly to "the joint and equal sovereigns of this country." Jay affirmed the "great and glorious principle, that the people are the sovereign of this country, and consequently that fellow citizens and joint sovereigns cannot be degraded by appearing with each other in their own Courts to have their controversies determined." In this discussion, Jay refers to "that popular sovereignty in which every citizen partakes," clearly connecting the conception of individual sovereignty to the concept of popular sovereignty.

Justices Wilson's and Jay's individualist conception of popular sovereignty present the radical yet fundamental idea that if anyone is sovereign, it is "We the People" as individuals, in the citizenry as a whole, rather than in a majority of the electorate.

## Our Republican Constitution

What are the implications of adopting an individual rather than a collective conception of popular sovereignty? I contend that an individual conception of popular sovereignty yields a Republican rather than a Democratic Constitution.

Under the Republican Constitution, because "the People" consists of each and every person, the power to govern must be delegated to some *subset* of the people. This small subset of the people who are empowered to govern are not to be confused with the people themselves, but are considered to be mere **servants** of the people. The people are the principals or masters and those in government merely their agents. As agents, they are to govern on behalf of the people and are subject to its ultimate control.

To ensure these servants remain within what the Declaration called their "just powers," however, under the Republican Constitution this law-making power must *itself* be limited by law. The Republican Constitution, then, provides the *law that governs those who govern us* and it is put in writing so it can be enforced against the servants of the people, each of whom must swear a solemn oath to obey "this Constitution."

Those servants or agents who swear the oath to "*this* Constitution"—the written one—can no more change the "law that governs them" than we can change the speed limits that are imposed *on us*. In short, under the Republican Constitution, *the meaning of the written Constitution must*

> **The Republican Constitution provides the *law that governs those who govern us*, and it is put in writing so it can be enforced against the servants of the people, each of whom must swear a solemn oath to obey 'this Constitution.'**

*remain the same until it is properly changed*—which is another way of saying that the written Constitution must be interpreted according to its original meaning until it is properly amended.

Under the Republican Constitution, judges too are servants of the people who have a *duty* to adhere to the law of the Constitution above any statute enacted by Congress or by the states. Judges are given life-time tenure precisely so they may hold legislatures *within the proper scope of their just powers* and (by so doing) protect the individual "rights . . . retained by the people"—and "the privileges or immunities of citizens"—from being denied, disparaged, or abridged by their servants in the legislature.

## Is Ours a Republican Constitution?

So do we have a Republican or a Democratic Constitution? I suggest that what I am calling our Republican Constitution began with the Declaration of Independence, which stated that *first come rights and then comes government*, and it is "to secure these rights," that governments are instituted among men. So the proper measure of any government is how well it protects the natural and inalienable rights to life, liberty, and the pursuit of happiness.

But the Articles of Confederation only imperfectly implemented the individual popular sovereignty expressed in the Declaration. State governments were dominated by legislatures, some elected annually, with weak executives and subordinate judges. As popularly elected state legislatures enacted measures that undermined the rights of the minority to benefit the majority of voters, and enacted laws that protected in-state businesses from out-of-state competition, the economy languished.

To address these problems, a new and more Republican Constitution—based on revised "republican" principles—was devised in Philadelphia to provide for a more perfect union.

To better secure the natural rights of the sovereign people, states were barred from impairing the obligations of contract or interfering with interstate commerce, or commerce with foreign nations. These and other powers were placed in the hands of a new form of national government.

The powers of this national government were then divided into three separate and co-equal branches, each of which was to check and balance the others. Law-making power was to be separate from its enforcement, and an independent judiciary was empowered to ensure that all three branches played by the rules laid down in the Republican Constitution. And the lawmaking power of Congress was limited to those powers "herein granted" in a written Constitution to which all must take an oath to uphold. Our Republican Constitution was put in writing to assure that it cannot be forgotten.

Unfortunately, even the "new and improved" Republican Constitution was incomplete. Southern states continued to maintain their tyrannical and unjust rule by the majority—or in some states even by a minority—over their slaves, whose pre-existing rights to life, liberty, and the pursuit of happiness were altogether denied. Eventually a new Republican Party with an expressly antislavery agenda arose and supplanted the Whigs. In just six years, it captured the presidency and control of Congress, which induced the Southern slave states to secede from the Union, taking those they held in bondage with them

After the Civil War ended slavery by force of arms, the Republicans in the Thirty-eighth Congress drafted and secured ratification of the Thirteenth Amendment to forever abolish slavery, even in states that had previously allowed it, and gave Congress the enumerated power to enforce this abolition. But winning the war and amending the Constitution was not enough. Southern racists resisted the new constitutional order, engaging in a brutal campaign of public and private terrorism.

So the Republicans proposed two new amendments that would finally complete our Republican Constitution. The Fourteenth Amendment would protect the privileges and immunities of U.S. citizens from being abridged by the legislative, judicial, and executive branches of their own states. Then, when the incentives in the Fourteenth Amendment for black suffrage proved inadequate, the Republicans drafted and secured the ratification of the Fifteenth Amendment to guarantee the right of blacks to vote.

Sadly, all these efforts to complete the Republican Constitution were stymied by the Supreme Court. In case of after case, the Court gutted one provision after the other, effectively nullifying key provisions of the written Constitution itself. It was no coincidence, therefore, that it was in the 1890 case of *Hans v. Louisiana* that the Supreme Court declared that the Eleventh Amendment had repudiated *Chisholm v. Georgia* in favor of the principle of state sovereignty. Then, just six years later in *Plessy v. Ferguson*, the Court completely deferred to the sovereign states using their police powers to segregate the races supposedly to ensure the public order.

It was not until 1952, in *Brown v. Board of Education*, that the Supreme Court, led by Republican Earl Warren, who had been nominated to be Chief Justice by Republican Dwight Eisenhower, led a unanimous Court to invalidate popularly enacted racial segregated schools, which was then followed by the gradual invalidation of all forms of racial segregation. Together with new federal civil and voting rights acts, these court rulings constituted a "second Reconstruction" that finally redeemed the Republican Constitution's promise that the rights of the individual must take precedence over the collective will of the people as manifested by a majority of the electorate.

## Protecting the Sovereignty of the People

It is no coincidence that the textual provisions of the Constitution that recognize the individualist nature of popular sovereignty have had to be ignored to make our Constitution more democratic.

Take the Ninth Amendment, which affirms that "[t]he enumeration in the Constitution, of certain rights, shall not be construed to deny or disparage others retained by the people." We know these rights are retained by the people *as individuals* because the Ninth Amendment was added to prevent construing the other individual rights that were enumerated in the Bill of Rights as the only rights the people have.

The Tenth Amendment affirms that "[t]he powers not delegated to the United States by the Constitution, nor prohibited by it to the states, are reserved to the states respectively, or to the people." The Constitution acknowledges that the people may retain powers as well as rights, and it expressly distinguishes the people from the states.

And the Fourteenth Amendment says, "No state shall make or enforce any law which shall abridge the privileges or immunities of citizens of the United States," which altered our system of federalism to create a power in Congress and the federal courts to protect the privileges or immunities of citizens from being abridged by their own state legislatures.

But what are these individual rights that are retained by the people? The idea of individual popular sovereignty helps us better to understand just what rights and powers, privileges and immunities are retained by the people. Under the Republican Constitution, the rights and powers retained by the people resemble those enjoyed by sovereign monarchs.

- Just as sovereign monarchs claim jurisdiction over their territories, sovereign individual citizens have jurisdiction over their private property.

- Just as one monarch may not interfere within the territorial jurisdiction of other monarchs, no citizen may interfere with the person and property of any other.
- Just as monarchs may consensually alter their legal relations with other monarchs by entering into treaties, so too may individual citizens freely alter their legal relations with their "fellow citizens and joint-sovereigns" by entering into contracts with each other.

Of course, the Republican Constitution is established, in part, so that these liberties of the individual may be regulated by law. But the proper purpose of such regulation must be limited to the *equal protection of the rights of each and every person*—as the Equal Protection Clause expressly affirmed. Any law that does not have *this* as its purpose is beyond the just powers of a republican legislature. In short, when the liberty of a "fellow citizen and joint sovereign" is restricted, judges as agents of the people have a judicial duty to critically assess whether the legislature has improperly exceeded its just powers.

This does not entail that judges should be speculating about the "natural rights of man" either to restrict legislative power or to require that these judicially discovered rights be honored by the other branches. This is not what they have been trained as lawyers to do.

Instead of singling out special rights or special groups for special protections, judges should ensure that laws restricting the life, liberty, or property of any person has not been irrational, arbitrary, or discriminatory. The end of such measures must be articulated by the other branches, and then the means allegedly adopted to implement these ends must be critically assessed to ensure that they are neither unnecessary infringements on liberty nor improper efforts to enrich or benefit some at the expense of other fellow citizens and joint sovereigns. And judges should also independently assess whether Congress has exceeded its enumerated powers or has delegated too much of its power to the executive branch.

**Where We Stand Today**

Today we live in a world in which most people adhere to aspects of both the Republican and Democratic Constitutions. Sometimes, they favor the "will of the people," and other times they urge the protection of individual rights. Much intellectual effort has been expended to make this combination coherent, but ultimately these two positions cannot coexist. Their inherent incoherence contributes to the opportunistic assertion of "the will of the people" when it favors one's policy positions and the rights of individuals to be free of "the tyranny of the majority" when it does not.

But in recent years, we have witnessed a growing sympathy for reviving and renewing our Republican Constitution's commitment to the sovereignty of the people, as individuals. Only by recognizing the difference between the Democratic Constitution and the Republican Constitution can we ever hope to recapture the benefits that have distinguished the American form of constitutionalism from that of other countries. The benefit of realizing that first come the rights of the people as individuals, and only then comes government as their servant. The benefit of realizing that the will of the majority is not the solution to the problem of constitutional legitimacy but *is the problem a republican form of government is needed to solve.* For only a Republican Constitution like ours can, if followed, secure the sovereignty of the people—each and every one.

4

# THE CLASSICAL LIBERAL TRADITION OF SOUND MONEY

By Lawrence H. White

---

**The fourth Liggio Lecture was delivered on September 24, 2016, at Atlas Network's Liberty Forum in Miami, in the wake of the 40th General Meeting of the Mont Pelerin Society.**

**At the time, Atlas Network had a Project of Sound Money that had been inaugurated some years earlier with a booklet, *A Guide to Sound Money*, by economist Judy Shelton, featuring a Hayek quote that Leonard brought up in our first meeting with Judy: "All those who wish to stop the drift toward increasing government control should concentrate their efforts on monetary policy."**

**Larry White used his Liggio Lecture to go deep on this subject, which had been of great interest to Leonard. Larry is a professor of economics at George Mason University, a distinguished senior fellow of the F. A. Hayek Program for Advanced Study in Philosophy, Politics, and Economics of the Mercatus Center at George Mason University, and a senior scholar of the Cato Institute Center for Monetary and Financial Alternatives.**

---

Let me welcome you all to the capital of Latin America. And when I say capital, I mean that much of the financial wealth of Latin America is held with banks and fund managers across the street, here in Miami. And therein lies a lesson in the results of unsound money.

But seriously, I am very pleased to be this year's Leonard Liggio lecturer. I thank Atlas Network and especially Brad Lips and Alex Chafuen for the honor.

## The Classical Liberal Tradition of Sound Money

I knew Leonard Liggio for forty years. I first met him in the fall of 1974 at the "Libertarian Scholars' Conference" in New York City. I last spoke to him on the phone in 2014, when he was ill but still hopeful of recovering and resuming his travels to conferences on behalf of Atlas Network.

I want to tell one story about Leonard before I turn to my topic. While I was in college, I somehow became responsible for organizing an extracurricular evening lecture that Leonard was to give on our campus. The topic was the historical background to the civil war then raging in Angola. The lecture was scheduled to last one hour. Leonard had no notes with him. But that's not the best part. As we walked to the lecture hall, Leonard turned and asked me, "Should I start the history around 1400 or 1900?" As though I knew something about Angola's history. I improvised a reply: "Why don't you start around 1400, and try to get to 1900 within the first 20 minutes, then bring it up to the present?" He said okay, and proceeded to do just that.

I want to talk this evening about the tradition of classical liberal thought on sound money. Don't worry, I won't start around 1400.

That's too late. I will start around 1350. I do, however, have notes.

How do the principles of classical liberalism apply to money? Pretty much as they do to wheat. They call for allowing users and suppliers of money to interact in a market system free of state *privileges*, free of *legal restrictions*, other than those against fraud and theft, and free of discretionary *regulatory* controls.

But money is more important than wheat, and I don't say that in a spirit of gluten intolerance. Some of you may recall the *Simpsons* episode where Homer drops a peanut that disappears between the cushions of his sofa. Fishing for it, he finds a $20 bill. "Aw, twenty dollars?" he says, "I wanted a peanut." Homer's brain immediately tells him: "Twenty dollars can buy many peanuts." "Explain how!" Homer demands. His brain answers: "Money can be exchanged for goods and services."

As the commonly accepted medium of exchange, money is the good on one side of every transaction. State disruptions to the supply of money, or to the demand for money, boggle not just one market but the entire economy. Historically, one of the oldest abridgements of economic freedom is the state's monopoly over the mint. It goes back to ancient times, because as soon as merchants developed the technology of coinage, mint monopoly could provide a major source of revenue. Because state abuse of coinage is so ancient, it was a leading-edge issue on which the ideas of economic liberalism began to form.

The scope for private institutions to supply money grew during the Middle Ages as commercial banks provided a *better* money than the royal mints. But today private money production and use is heavily circumscribed by laws and regulations. You and I are restricted in how we can spend and transfer the money we own. The little freedom that remains is under attack. For example, the Harvard economist Kenneth Rogoff has a new book entitled *The Curse of Cash*, in which he calls for the abolition of $20 and $100 bills because—hold on to your seat—criminals use them. Not to be outdone, Prof. Narayan Kocherlakota, former president of the Federal Reserve Bank of Minneapolis, published an opinion piece earlier this month calling for the federal government to "abolish currency and move completely to electronic cash." There are similar moves afoot in Europe.

And those are just the intellectuals. The actual regulators at the U.S. Treasury Department's Financial Crimes Enforcement Network are scarier still. They not only abridge the financial privacy rights of Americans, they pressure governments around the world to adopt the intrusive U.S. "know your customer" rules if they want to do business with any U.S. banks.

I was fortunate that Leonard Liggio helped to direct my reading in the history of money and the history of liberalism as it relates to money. In particular he drew my attention to work by the early French scholastic writer Nicole Oresme, from the 1350s, and to the works of the twentieth-century economic historian Raymond de Roover. (Has anyone else here experienced the majesty that is de Roover's article "What Is Dry Exchange?") In an autobiographical essay, Leonard recalled having talked for "hours with de Roover over beer" after a meeting of the monthly Mises circle in New York at which de Roover had come to give a presentation.

De Roover, by the way, famously debunked the "fairy tale" (his words) that the Christian scholars of the Middle Ages, the Scholastics, subscribed to a cost-of-production theory of the "just price." Instead, for most of them, the "just price" was simply the prevailing market price, absent collusion or emergency. (Since Alex Chafuen is here, I thought I'd throw in a good word for the Scholastics.)

Some of the earliest Christian thinkers up to 1225, however, took an actively hostile view toward money. One reads that the Franciscan and Dominican religious orders, founded in 1209 and 1216, initially refused even to handle coins. For them money was either sinful as such, or at least posed a temptation. Then Aristotle's *Nichomachean Ethics* was rediscovered and disseminated across Europe. It introduced into Scholastic thought the idea that money is so useful that it actually promotes society's well-being. But Aristotle's writings on money were highly equivocal. The Philosopher, as the Scholastics called him, had declared on the one hand that money had naturally arisen as a convenient measure of value, but on the other hand that it "exists not by nature but by law."

Thomas Aquinas didn't have all that much to say about money. The key early Scholastic work on money was by Nicole (or Nicholas) Oresme (c.1320–82), a French bishop, who drew on his teacher, Jean Buridan. F. A. Hayek once commented that "Italy of the sixteenth century has been called the country of the worst money and the best monetary theory." France of the fourteenth century is a close contender. Buridan and Oresme lived through, and were outraged by, a massive debasement of the French coinage by King Philip the Fair. Or perhaps we should call him Philip the Unfair.

Oresme's great work, published around 1358, has been called "the first text dedicated solely to money and particularly to the alteration of coins." The monograph, in Latin, has a long Latin title that means "Treatise on the origin, nature, law, and alteration of monies." It also goes by a shorter title: *De Moneta*, "On money." In a recent account, the scholar Fabian Wittreck comments that Oresme wrote it not in a mood of serene scholarly detachment but in a "desperate attempt to influence the monetary policy of his prince."

A few years back (2000) I had the opportunity to edit a three-volume collection of historical writings entitled *The History of Gold and Silver*. I naturally led off volume 1 with an English translation of Oresme's *De Moneta*.

Here is Oresme's argument in a nutshell: Coins held by ordinary people are their own property, not the king's property. The people are defrauded when the state mint dishonestly debases the coins.[1] Fraud is unjust. Hence, if the sovereign runs the mint,

> **Oresme's argument in a nutshell: Coins held by ordinary people are their own property, not the king's property. The people are defrauded when the state mint dishonestly debases the coins.**

---

1  Technical aside: there are three ways to debase: [1] remint coins with a lower percentage silver content, using the same coin dies and giving them the same face value;

the sovereign is duty-bound not to debase. If he debases, he acts unjustly. He cheats the people.

This was radical talk. Oresme's work was a landmark in the development of the view that the sovereign and the state officials are not above the law, but answerable to it. The actions of state agents are illegitimate if they violate the sacred rights of the people.

Oresme and his followers were not modern libertarians, of course. They accepted the sovereign's monopoly in coin production that they lived under. Oresme even commented that fraud would be a danger if unofficial parties could make coins. (This reminds me of Milton Friedman's one-time view, which he later revised, that fraud would be a danger if unofficial parties could issue banknotes. I will return to this later.) Oresme did not consider whether competition among mints—not entirely unknown in France at the time—might actually be more effective than sovereign control of a monopoly mint as a means for restraining fraudulent practices. Today, we actually have numismatic evidence that it was. In the gold and silver rushes of the American West, private mints (at least, the ones that survived) were *more* scrupulous. Their coins were more precisely minted than official coins. Their business more keenly depended on it.

Oresme had great influence, particularly on the important German scholastic Gabriel Biel, who wrote in the late 1400s, and on the outstanding Spanish scholastic Juan de Mariana, who wrote in the early 1600s. Mariana is of course more famous of the two today because he has an Atlas Network-linked institute named after him, founded by Gabriel Calzada and now directed by Juan Ramon Rallo. As far as I am aware, there is no Gabriel Biel Institute. It's a pity.

---

[2] reduce the coins' weight without reducing their face value, and [3] "cry up" the currency, i.e., raise the face value of existing coins with no change in content.

Biel observed that a sovereign who dishonestly reduces the silver content of coins when minting or re-minting them, without any necessity, but only to make a profit, acts no differently from a low-life individual who alters coins by filing or sweating them. Such a sovereign commits a mortal sin. He is a cheat; he bears false witness. The alteration is an act of tyranny, since it is an unjust exaction on the people.

Juan de Mariana extended Oresme's analysis in his work *De Monetae Mutatione (On the Alteration of Money)*, published a few years after the debasement of small-denomination copper coins by King Philip III of Spain in 1602. In the Castilian Spanish of the day, the copper coins were called *vellones*, which also meant "fleeces" from sheep—appropriately, because the coins quickly became a device by which the king *fleeced* the public.

Mariana distinguished the just king from the tyrant this way: "The tyrant is he who tramples everything underfoot and believes that everything belongs to him." The just king, by contrast, respects the property rights of the people. As Mariana charmingly put it, a just king "limits his covetousness within the terms of reason and justice." It follows that the just king may not debase the coinage without the consent of the people, nor may he tax them, nor impose monopolies, without their consent.

To drive the point home, Mariana reasonably asked: "Look: would it be allowed for a prince to break into his subjects' granaries, take half of the grain stored there for himself, and by way of compensation allow the owners to sell the remainder at the same price as the original whole?" And he answers: "I do not think that there would be anyone so preposterous as to condone such an act. But that is precisely what happened with the old copper coins."

This was *very* radical talk. Verging on treason, even.

The legal historian Wim Decock (2016) relates that Mariana "was held in custody in Madrid and Rome, and was urged to modify offensive passages in his treatise. In the meantime, Pope Paul V put the first edition of *De Monetae Mutatione* (1609) on the Spanish Index of prohibited books. Moreover, state officials removed almost all extant copies from circulation."

Mariana referred to debasements as "tricks," and warned that they "are geared towards one and the same unlawful end, namely to oppress the people with new burdens and to amass money." In 1776, Adam Smith likewise referred to debasement as a "juggling trick," whereby a government pretends to repay its debts in coin but actually defaults on them by paying less in precious metal than is owed.[2]

Inspired by writers like these, classical liberalism coalesced around opposition to rule by unconstrained authorities. Or to put it positively, liberal thinkers learned to uphold individual liberty and private property rights, including freedom of contract, under the rule of law.

From the late Scholastics, let's now fast-forward 150 years to the Scottish Enlightenment, where the two most important defenders of monetary liberalism were David Hume and Adam Smith. The anti-liberal or Mercantilist writers of the day advised the sovereign to have the nation perpetually run a so-called balance of trade "surplus"—sell more exports, buy fewer imports—in order to perpetually accumulate silver and gold. Hume demonstrated—through one of the first uses of explicit thought experiments in economics—that this mercantilist advice was foolishness.

The "price-specie flow mechanism" spelled out by Hume shows how the quantity of silver or gold in an economy regulates itself. When the domestic public has less money than it wants, they

---

2  On the Spanish scholastics more generally, see Marjorie Grice-Hutchinson, *Early Economic Thought in Spain, 1177–1740* (1978), and of course, Alejandro Chafuen, *Faith and Liberty: The Economic Thought of the Late Scholastics* (2003).

soon enough get more by retaining some of the money that flows in through sales of goods to the rest of the world, accumulating it rather than spending it off by buying imports, until the public builds up its money balances to the desired size. Conversely, money balances in excess of the desired quantity flow out, through purchases of goods and services that are more highly desired at the margin. The national or regional stock of metallic money thus regulates itself through market forces. Import quotas or taxes, and export subsidies, are completely unneeded to keep the economy fully stocked with metallic money.

Adam Smith extended Hume's argument: self-regulation *also* governs the regional quantity of a "mixed currency" consisting of silver or gold coins *plus* redeemable banknotes issued by competing commercial banks, the system that surrounded him in Scotland. He saw other benefits in the Scottish system of "free banking." First, the voluntary use of redeemable notes and transferable deposits offered by competing banks, as a substitute for precious metal coins, enhanced the wealth of the nation, allowing the export of some of the coin stock to finance the import of productive machines. Smith argued that "the greater part" of the gold and silver sent abroad will "almost unavoidabl[y]" be used to "purchase an additional stock of materials, tools, and provisions" that is "destined for the employment of industry." Banknotes thus enabled the nation to exchange much of its "dead stock" of gold and silver for productive capital goods.

Smith saw another major benefit of free banking: having note-issue decentralized provided diversification against risk of default by a currency issuer. If one bank out of twenty defaults, 5 percent of the public suffers. By contrast, if a monopoly issuer like the Bank of England defaults, everyone suffers, and the metallic standard is suspended for everyone. As Smith wrote in the *Wealth of Nations*:

> The late multiplication of banking companies in both parts of the United Kingdom, an event by which many people have been much alarmed, instead of diminishing, increases the security of the public. . . . By dividing the whole circulation into a greater number of parts, the failure of any one company, an accident which, in the course of things, must sometimes happen, becomes of less consequence to the public.

Already in 1776, Smith had identified the remedy for "too big to fail" banks: allow free entry and grant no privileges. And a remedy to the problem of the untrustworthiness of central banks: have money issued by *many* firms *bound by contract to redeem*, not by one body that is above the law.

Finally, Smith saw advantages in free competition among banks in lending: better terms for their customers. He concluded:

> This free competition, too, obliges all bankers to be more liberal in their dealings with their customers, lest their rivals should carry them away. In general, if any branch of trade, or any division of labour, be advantageous to the public, the freer and more general the competition, it will always be the more so.

One of Hume's and Smith's prominent followers, the English classical economist Nassau Senior, in an 1827 lecture rightly ridiculed

> that extraordinary monument of human absurdity, the Mercantile Theory,—or, in other words, the opinion that wealth consists of gold and silver, and may be indefinitely increased by forcing their importation, and preventing their exportation: a theory which has occasioned, and still occasions, more vice, misery, and war, than all other errors put together.

On this side of the Atlantic, we know that Founding Father Alexander Hamilton—he of the $10 bill and the smash Broadway hit—read *The Wealth of Nations*. And yet he promoted monopoly privileges for the Bank of the United States in 1791. He was unfortunately a mercantilist in banking policy as well as in trade policy. Although Ben Bernanke has written that Hamilton "was without doubt the best and most foresighted economic policymaker in U.S. history," I reply, "Not!" Hamilton had an essentially mercantilist agenda, and failed to embrace the better and more foresighted liberal policies that Smith laid before him.

Thomas Jefferson, Hamilton's great opponent on economic policy, also read Adam Smith, but in his own way also failed to embrace Smith's teachings. While Jefferson rightly opposed Hamilton's single federally privileged nationwide bank of issue, he favored *zero* nationwide banks of issue, not many. He was even suspicious of state-government-chartered banks of issue.

Smith's work on banking did, however, come to inspire defenders of "free banking" around the world in the debates that surrounded the creation of national central banks in the nineteenth and twentieth centuries. (A classic account of these debates is Vera Smith's *The Rationale of Central Banking*, published 1936. It is available at the Liberty Fund's website.) In Britain there was what I call a "Free Banking School" in the 1825–50 period who argued for removing rather than enhancing the Bank of England's monopoly privileges. Smith's followers in the FBS strengthened his arguments for free trade in banking and for viewing bank-issued money as self-regulating. On the Continent, Jean-Baptiste Say and others recommended free banking over central banking.

Here in the United States classical liberals like William Leggett and Richard Hildreth in the 1830s argued for free entry into banking and note-issue rather than the restrictive chartering system in place. In Latin American countries, periods of liberal constitutions during the nineteenth century often brought free banking reforms, enacted as an integral part of liberal economic policy. (By the way, a new volume on Chile's favorable experience with free banking will soon be published by scholars at the Universidad de Desarollo.) All these advocates saw that free banking is the policy ideal that results from applying the norms of classical liberalism to money and banking.

Other leading classical liberals of the nineteenth century, I regret to note, failed to consistently apply their principles to money. David Ricardo favored nationalization of coinage and banknote issue, and the forced substitution of redeemable paper notes for coins in all but the largest payments. Richard Cobden, the heroic leader of the movement against the Corn Law tariffs, supported the nationalization of banknotes.

Whereas Smith and Hume largely shied away from analyzing whether the sovereign's policy was unjust or sinful, and asked mainly whether it was prudent, two of their followers were quite passionate: Thomas Paine in the 1780s and William Cobbett in the 1810s.

Paine took up the theme of the bane of irredeemable government-issued paper as against the blessing of gold and gold-redeemable banknotes. The occasion was a threat, soon after the Revolutionary War ended, that the Commonwealth of Pennsylvania would issue its own irredeemable paper notes. Like Adam

Smith, Paine recognized the benefits of redeemable commercial banknotes. He warned:

> But when an assembly undertake to issue paper as money, the whole system of safety and certainty is overturned, and property set afloat. Paper notes given and taken between individuals as a promise of payment is one thing, but paper issued by an assembly as money is another thing. It is like putting an apparition in the place of a man; it vanishes with looking at it, and nothing remains but the air.

Like Oreseme and Mariana before him, Paine denounced the injustice of legal tenders laws that compel creditors to accept payment in legally overvalued money worth a fraction in the market of the money repayment actually contracted for. He declared:

> As to the assumed authority of any assembly in making paper money, or paper of any kind, a legal tender, or in other language, a compulsive payment, it is a most presumptuous attempt at arbitrary power. There can be no such power in a republican government: the people have no freedom, and property no security where this practice can be acted. . . . If anything had or could have a value equal to gold and silver, it would require no tender law; and if it had not that value it ought not to have such a law; and, therefore, all tender laws are tyrannical and unjust and calculated to support fraud and oppression.

I have been fortunate in my career to have a second mentor besides Leonard, namely Walter Grinder, who worked with Leonard for many years at the Institute for Humane Studies. When I told Walter a few weeks ago what the theme of this talk would be, he urged me to include the English writer William Cobbett among the liberal heroes on the money question. Cobbett's most famous work on money was *Paper against Gold*, first published in 1810 during a period in which the Bank of England had stopped redeeming its notes in gold or silver. (Liberty Fund now carries *Paper against Gold* [1815 edition] in its Online Library of Liberty.)

Like Paine, Cobbett was passionate about the injustice of what he called "that dreadful curse, a paper-money not convertible into gold and silver." He roundly condemned the hypocrisy of Parliamentary defenders of the Bank's continued breach of contract: "You tell us that the public like Bank notes as well as guineas [gold coins]. But, with these assertions upon your lips, you pass a *law* to protect the Bank against the demands of that public; you pass a law to *compel* that public to receive paper at the Bank, instead of that gold, which you say they like no better than that paper."

One of the best pieces of advice I ever received came from Walter Grinder forty years ago, when I had to write a paper for a college course in U.S. intellectual history. He recommended that I look into the writings of William Leggett, the most free-market thinker of the Jacksonian Era. It was in Legget's work that I first saw a reference to the experience of free banking in Scotland, which became the subject of my dissertation and first book. I'm still milking the topic. So I'd say Walter's tip paid off handsomely. (I also edited a collection of Leggett's writings for Liberty Fund, now available online.)

Leggett, a journalist in New York City in the 1830s, was a key intellectual mover behind the so-called "Free Banking" laws adopted in various states. So-called, because they did not institute anything close to laissez-faire in banking, although they did open up and regularize the process of obtaining incorporation for banks. For Leggett, the injustice of restricting entry into banknote issuing followed from the principle that any individual "has a natural right to give his promise to pay a certain sum on a piece of paper, and, subscribing it with his name, to pass it for what those with whom he deals may be willing to receive it."

Leggett's ideal was the complete separation of government from involvement with banking. He opposed both government sponsorship of banks and, unlike some hard-money Jacksonians, equally opposed any legislative ban on privately issued banknotes, writing that "an exclusive metallick currency could only be instituted and maintained by the force of arbitrary government edicts, totally contrary to the first principles of natural justice."

Competition among banks will ensure that the public receives whatever security against fraud it demands: "Let existing banks be subject to unrestricted competition, and then the banking associations, whether corporate or voluntary, that give the public the largest securities, and conduct their affairs with the wisest economy, will meet with the greatest success." All that governments need to do is to "repeal those enactments which forbid the free use of capital and credit." In his endorsement of full laissez-faire in the provision of bank money Leggett went beyond Adam Smith, who had endorsed a ban on small notes and a ban on contractual clauses that gave banks the option to delay redemption on banknotes (for a penalty).

When restriction of the right of note issue was defended by analogy to the federal government's constitutional power of coinage, Leggett was led by the logic of free trade to stand the argument on its head: "we have our doubts . . . whether it would not be better to leave coinage as well as banking, entirely to the laws of trade."

Let's skip ahead one more time. In the twentieth century the Austrian economist Ludwig von Mises reformulated the case for free banking with new analytical rigor in his great work *The Theory of Money and Credit* (1912). Friedrich Hayek made somewhat ambivalent cases for gold and free banking earlier in his career (in his 1937 book *Monetary Nationalism and International Stability*), but in the 1970s called forcefully for *Choice in Currency* and then *The Denationalisation of Money*.

Mises and Hayek were of course founding members of the Mont Pelerin Society. Many other members, led by Milton Friedman, had made peace with central banking and fiat money during the 1940s through the 1970s. I'm told that debates over the gold standard versus rule-bound fiat money raged for so many years within the society, without resolution, that the topic has been deliberately omitted from the program since the 1980s.

Leonard Liggio described Milton Friedman's early position in this way when he wrote a piece summarizing the monetary debate at the 1978 Mont Pelerin Society meetings: "Friedman said . . . that he believed government intervention in money was inevitable, and that therefore, the proper role of an economist was to advocate sensible interventions. He . . . advocated a constitutional amendment which would establish the rules that the monetary authority should follow. Friedman insisted that 'We are doomed' if we believe that de-statizing money is the only answer." Leonard's narrative continues: "F. A. Hayek then rose from the audience. . . . He noted that the gold standard historically was the only discipline on governments. He reaffirmed his own opposition to all monopoly on money and to all government control of money. He presented what he calls his revolutionary program—monetary competition in each country after denationalization or destatization of money. The private issue of money, he argued, is the only answer."

It should be noted that Friedman moved toward Hayek's denationalization direction in the 1980s. I personally became aware of this change of outlook in 1983. In that year I published a piece in the *Cato Journal*, which in one passage criticized Friedman's 1960 book *A Program for Monetary Stability*, and his 1962 *Capitalism and Freedom*, where he endorsed government monopoly of currency (on the grounds that private currency is inherently fraud-prone) and called for certain bank regulations to make control of the monetary aggregates easier for the Fed. Professor Friedman kindly sent me a note about that passage, telling me that our views were not as different as I thought. In a 1984 piece he called for freezing the monetary liabilities of the central bank, shutting down the central bank's monetary policy committee, and allowing private competition in currency issue to satisfy any growth in the public's demand for currency.

**What had changed Friedman's mind? Evidence.**

What had changed Friedman's mind? Evidence. The post-1962 research on free banking by Hugh Rockoff and others had persuaded him that inherent fraud was not a problem with private note-issue, while his own frustration in getting the Fed to adopt a rule (interpreted in the light of public choice arguments) had convinced him that a central bank would wriggle around any rule imposed on it so long as it continued to exist. In a 1986 piece co-authored with Anna Schwartz he was ready to give a more classical liberal answer to the question posed in the piece's title: "Has Government Any Role in Money?"

This is the question I want to leave you with: If we want to enlarge monetary freedom, and limit the government's role in the monetary system in the interest of sounder money, what's the best way for us to do that?

5

# REDISCOVERING POLITICAL IDEALS

*By David Schmidtz*

---

The COVID-19 pandemic forced Atlas Network to hold its 2020 Liberty Forum virtually, so the Liggio Lecture of that year was pre-recorded and broadcast alongside other live and interactive sessions on November 11, 2020.

During a moment of extreme political polarization, David Schmidtz identified a failure of philosophy as a root problem to 2020's raging polarization and departure from norms of civil discourse. His 2020 Liggio Lecture explored how moral philosophy devolved from David Hume's and Adam Smith's empirical studies of human cooperation to mere intuitions about fairness. He pointed a way to again foster interdisciplinary study of what it takes for people to live together successfully. David is Kendrick Professor of Philosophy and Eller Chair of Service-Dominant Logic at the University of Arizona.

---

I'm going to talk tonight about moral philosophy as it emerged from the Scottish Enlightenment at the end of the 1700s. Towering over the Enlightenment, David Hume and Adam Smith were on a quest to introduce the experimental method of reasoning into moral subjects, to borrow the subtitle of Hume's treatise. Things didn't go according to plan though, and therein lies a story.

To be clear, while I'm going to talk about a feature of the academy that I regret, I have no personal complaint. Things have gone well. I've had fabulous mentors, one of whom was Leonard Liggio. Leonard had an extraordinary career and was blessed with some great colleagues. He was an awesome scholar. He did it the right way. He sweated the details. And he put together incredible narratives stuffed with detail. If you've ever heard

Leonard lecture, you know what I'm talking about. Leonard also had a moral compass and a big heart, but he was shy. I had many conversations with him when I was a student, but he was so low-key, I'd ask him a question, he'd answer in detail, with footnotes, and that was the end of the conversation. That's all I got from him in terms of reaction or recognition, so I wasn't sure that he even knew who I was.

But then I got my first overseas invitation, and that's how I met Jacques and Pierre Garello in Aix-en-Provence in 1988. Then I got my second overseas invitation, this time to Dubrovnik in 1989, just before the fall of the Berlin Wall, and everyone knew the world was going to change. Both of those invitations were quietly instigated by Leonard Liggio. And Leonard was tickled. He knew those would be formative events for me, and he knew I'd never forget. So I didn't know Leonard well, but I knew him well enough that I can thank him for showing me what kind of man a scholar can be. And I won't forget that either.

So thanks so much, Brad and everyone, for having me here and for joining us at this event. It's one of the great honors of my career. Now, let me try to connect a few historical dots in a way that I hope would've intrigued Leonard.

For those Scottish Enlightenment scholars, the mid-1700s was a heady time. Europe had never seen a better opportunity to make progress. Hume and Smith were pushing the frontier of moral science. Among philosophers, the Scottish observation-based approach was called "empiricism." The Enlightenment view was that there is such a thing as human nature. It can be studied and understood. The point is not that anything like the human condition is logically necessary. It's not something you deduce from axioms like a proof in geometry. The point is that, in crucial ways, the human condition is law-like. There are regularities. Certainty? It's not in the cards. But we can have grounds for making predictions.

To a scientist, having a basis for prediction doesn't mean we'll never be surprised. The point is that science and the predictability of things helps us to understand what to *count* as a surprise. We can know when the world is off script and trying to teach us something new. But it's also true that the ambition of Hume and Smith would become, I think, a victim of its own success. Their advocacy of observation-based reasoning, and of specialization, incidentally, would lead in the 1800s, not to philosophy becoming the moral science they envisioned but rather to the social sciences splitting away from philosophy, becoming their own departmental silos, and leaving philosophy to reinvent itself as a discipline that was anything but empirical.

By the mid-1800s, John Stuart Mill would come to be seen as taking empiricism to the limit—arguing that everything we know comes to us by experience and experiment. Even propositions like two plus two equals four are learned by generalizing from observed results. In his day, Mill was visible and influential as an expositor of the new moral sciences. So Mill was taken seriously when, in service of making moral philosophy more scientific, he produced a series of works culminating in 1848 with the *Principles of Political Economy*. In those writings, Mill

> [Smith's and Hume's] advocacy of observation-based reasoning... would lead in the 1800s, not to philosophy becoming the moral science they envisioned but rather to the social sciences splitting away from philosophy... leaving philosophy to reinvent itself as a discipline that was anything but empirical.

separated the study of how goods are *produced* from the study of how goods are *distributed.* That's what you do for the sake of analytical rigor and tough-minded science. If two things can be separated, you separate them. How goods are produced is a question for these new departments of economics. How goods ought to be distributed is a question for philosophers, the ones who work on justice.

Now, as one of our favorite Arizona alumni, Kevin Vallier, notes, Mill also thought humanity had largely exhausted the frontier of technological progress. To be sure, the telegraph had been invented by 1837. So by 1848, many people could see that electricity's potential, especially regarding distance communication, was far from exhausted. Even at the time then, there was ample reason to doubt that a steady-state economy was around the corner and to doubt that better distribution was the only remaining avenue for substantial human progress. And yet, for whatever reason, Mill did expect the coming age to be an economic steady-state with relatively little news on the production side. Human progress would come via better distribution, not rising productivity, which made distribution the central topic. Today, we don't remember Mill pressing that unfortunate distinction, but it shaped our thinking so fundamentally that we can hardly imagine not treating production and distribution as separate topics.

Scottish Enlightenment philosophers like Hume and Smith studied historical patterns that to them were relevant to questions about ethics—say the ethics of trade barriers. But ethics was no longer anchored in observable consequences of alternative trade policies, consequences for unemployment rates or consumer prices that workers were paying. Ethics and political philosophy had turned into something else, something so far removed from science that today calling it "moral science" could seem oxymoronic. But sometimes what looks like two things is actually one, along the lines of the morning star and the evening star. If we presume to treat them as separate simply because they appear to be so, we make mistakes.

Ironically, in the aftermath of Hume's distinction between production and distribution, really pulling one question about how society works and what makes people good for each other—pulling that question into two half questions—philosophy retreated from what empiricism had been. And it was cut off from the scientific study of what makes some societies more productive than others. The remnants of philosophy were left to ask how we ought to distribute pie. By default, we were left to assume that since distribution is the question that got left to philosophers, distribution must be the question of justice.

Now, I want to ask you to consider not only how abstract but how deceptive it is to imagine a pie sitting there passively waiting for us to decide how to slice it. Treated in academic isolation, there is no testable answer to the question of how to divide that pie. We have only rival intuitions about the fairness of dividing the pie one way or another. When intuitions conflict, we have no tools to resolve the conflict, other than to look into what's wrong with people who see things differently. Undergraduates infer from our inability to settle the debate that it's all relative or all subjective. We know they're badly mistaken, but after a century of distancing ourselves from tools for constructing testable hypotheses, even our best attempts to steer students back toward verifiable truth seem more clever than wise.

> **We were left to assume that since distribution is the question that got left to philosophers, distribution must be the question of justice.**

Yet, there was a time when we knew that justice has roughly nothing to do with how we treat the pie and everything to do with how we treat bakers. If we set aside everything we've learned about the terms of engagement under which bakers are better off living together, under which they become good for each other, there's no testable answer to the question of how to divide the pie. We know justice isn't merely a matter of opinion, but we made it look that way when we started treating philosophy as outside the realm of empirical tests.

Philosophy is now something like this: we look at a snapshot of a busy intersection, and we don't want to think of it as a process because philosophers don't study process, that's for somebody else. We want to think of it as like a pie. So we take a snapshot, and we see how arbitrary it is that some people have red lights and other people have green lights. We focus exclusively on the snapshot because cause and effect, empirical generalizations about process that we study in sociology or economics or psychology, those are all autonomous social sciences. Today, what works is social science. What's fair, that's philosophy. Any judge trying to resolve conflict knows there's no truth about what is fair in abstraction of what works as a basis for people getting on with their lives. But what's obvious to any judge, and what would have been obvious to Smith and Hume, has come to be invisible inside the academic silo of philosophy.

So if we set aside social science and just look at a snapshot of social life at its busy intersections, where traffic is congested and conflicts of interest become apparent, then we can have a vision that's beyond the reach of testing and refutation. Namely, in an ideally just world, everyone would have a green light at the same time. That would be treating it like a pie. It would be gridlock. It wouldn't be prosperous. It wouldn't be peaceful. But it would be just. So would it? Would it really be just? How would we know?

What would count as evidence? How do we start picking up the tools of social science that used to be part of philosophy and apply them to this kind of case?

Let's say that to call something justice is to say something good about it. So what's good about justice? What does justice do as a way of managing an ongoing process for us? Consider that justice evolved among human beings as a device for managing traffic; literally managing traffic, metaphorically managing *commercial* traffic, and so on. We call that traffic management device "justice." Justice didn't evolve as a device for telling us what to want, what our destination should be. Although we have misconstrued it that way.

Instead, what we call justice evolved as a device for coping with a realization that if there's going to be an enduring peace, it starts with recognizing that everyone has their own right to live. And it starts with not wanting to be a threat to our neighbors. It starts with wanting to show respect by treating them as having the right and responsibility to decide for themselves what to want. Justice evolved as a device for conveying our mutual intention not to be in each other's way. And beyond that, it signaled a mutual intention to be positively useful, to be of service, to be a positive contributor to the life of our neighbors, to build places for ourselves as contributors to a community; playing roles that our partners can appreciate, that our neighbors can appreciate.

That leaves us needing to know what justice is. And needing to know what justice is means needing our beliefs about justice to not merely be untestable intuition but to somehow, some way, be grounded in observable fact. One thing we can say is that some kinds of equality, like everyone having a green light at the same time, that's a prescription for gridlock, as I said. But there are other kinds of equality, like simply learning to take turns. When you're next in line, "Then, sir, it's your turn." That doesn't look like equality when you take a snapshot of it, but waiting your turn like everyone else is a profoundly egalitarian institution. Justice isn't everything, but it's a foundation, and nearly everything we want from a community is built on that foundation.

So let me rephrase, and in the process stress, if justice has anything to do with effective traffic management, it's helping us to know what to expect from each other, helping us to know what we're warranted in demanding of each other. Then justice is all about the fact that we have different destinations. And let's ponder that for a second. Observe the extent of disagreement and diversity in society. Consider how idiosyncratic and incompatible our individual visions of perfection are, and thus how unfit any of our visions are to be a blueprint for a community. Part of the essence of toleration, of mature adulthood, of being fit to live in a community at all is acknowledging that it isn't our place to decide what other people are for.

Presupposed by all of this the most primordial political fact of all: namely, the fact that I'm not alone. I live among beings who decide for themselves. I may feel that people can't reasonably reject my deepest convictions about justice, but they can and they know it. And this fact makes politics what it is, and it makes justice what it is. Ideally, we want to coexist in peace with all of our neighbors, not only the ideal ones, not only the perfect ones, not only the agreeable ones. Realistic idealism aims to identify what, if anything, is observably enabling people to thrive under actual conditions, not merely ideal ones. When disagreement is inevitable, the political ideal is to make disagreement non-threatening, to make it safe to disagree. A fully adult political animal's ideal is not to win, but to avoid needing to win.

Honestly, taking into account the fact of diversity comes down to asking, "What terms of engagement are appropriate for people who don't even agree on which terms of engagement are appropriate?" The question isn't cute, it's the crux of the human condition. Rushing to treat our own intuitions about perfect justice as rationally compelling is a classic way of failing to rise to the level of seriousness that justice demands.

So I work on theory, on understanding and explaining theory. And I work on comparing theories to maps. A theory is just like a map. A theory is a map drawn with words. Think about it. Consider an implication: no map represents the only reasonable way of seeing the terrain. There's no such thing as the one compellingly correct way to draw the map. We'd be astounded if we had two cartography students working separately on mapping a terrain and they drew identical maps. It wouldn't happen. If we did, we'd be sure at least one of them cheated. And theorizing is like that as well. If you ask students to develop theories about the same topic, and if they don't know what answer you're looking for and end up thinking for themselves, they come up with different theories. Theorizing doesn't lead to consensus.

## The Difference between a Moral Ideal and a Political Ideal

Some ideals are moral ideals, but some ideals are political ideals. We recognize that many of the people with whom we're going to live and with whom we'd rather not be at war are people whose moral ideals are unlike ours. And so we make a political decision. We determine we're not going agree, and then we work to make sure that in those areas we don't need to. Does it matter that we have no consensus on destinations? In ordinary life, not much. In ordinary life, what matters far more is that we readily coordinate on norms of traffic management. We figure out what to expect from each other. We figure out how to stay out of each other's way. We hardly ever come to a mutual understanding about who has the superior destination. And yet, we have a robust history of readily reaching mutual understanding about who has the right of way.

Freedom of religion. It's one of humanity's greatest triumphs. You don't need to decide whether my choice of religion is a good choice; you only need to decide whether it's *my* choice. What won the day was not a religion but people seeing that religion didn't have to come up for debate. And what grew in the soil of religious freedom, I should say, it's more general than religious toleration. It's the whole of modern Western Civilization. It's what used to be called liberalism. Our greatest triumphs in learning to live together stem not from agreeing on what's correct but from agreeing to let people decide for themselves. When discussion isn't needed, that's a triumph in specifying terms of engagement. We make progress by defining jurisdictions that respect people who want and need to share the road, but neither want nor need to share or even discuss destinations.

And above all, no one has to accept being relegated to a category of persons whose destination is second class. Thriving communities minimize our need to justify our destination to others. Indeed, a traffic management system's utility lies in people not needing to justify themselves. We don't stop at intersections to justify destinations; we stop because it's someone else's turn, and that's all we need to know. And that's liberalism's original insight. We need to know who has the right of way, not who has the ideal destination.

> **Our greatest triumphs in learning to live together stem not from agreeing on what's correct but from agreeing to let people decide for themselves.**

Freedom of religion and freedom of speech are among our signature successes in learning how to live together. Liberalism, in its classic form, is in part a confidence that the greater the range of beliefs made to feel at home in a society, the more intellectually vibrant, materially prosperous, and morally progressive a society ultimately will be.

# 6

# THE FUTURE OF REGULATION: WHAT WE CAN LEARN FROM THE PAST

By Hon. Douglas H. Ginsburg

---

**Senior Circuit Judge Douglas H. Ginsburg was appointed to the United States Court of Appeals for the District of Columbia in 1986; he served as Chief Judge from 2001 to 2008. Judge Ginsburg is currently a professor of law at the Antonin Scalia Law School, George Mason University, and a visiting professor at the University College London, Faculty of Laws.**

**When he gave the Liggio Lecture in New York City on November 7, 2019, he was creating a PBS documentary series, *A More or Less Perfect Union*, which was shown on public television stations in 2020.**

---

Good morning, all. I am delighted to be here today giving this talk in honor of my friend, Leonard Liggio. Leonard was a scholar with few equals, an enormous repository of bibliographic references, and a champion of classical liberal ideas. As Leonard once said, "Politics is for ideas. It is a way to introduce ideas, or the consequences of ideas into national life: blocking bad legislation, bad decisions."[1] All too often, the bad decision being considered is to regulate competition in some industry, to the detriment of consumers.

Today I will speak about the American experience with regulation over the course of the twentieth century, with an eye

---

1  Leonard Liggio interview with Students for Liberty (2010), https://studentsforliberty.org/wp-content/uploads/2011/02/Leonard-Liggio-AFL-Interview.pdf.

towards lessons we should take with us into the future. I have chosen this subject specifically because this is an international forum, and every nation, with only a few exceptions, can learn from our mistakes.

## I. The Origins and Rise of Economic Regulation

During the first few decades of the twentieth century a significant portion of our economy—agriculture, finance, transportation, energy, and communications—was subjected to pervasive regulation that typically regulated prices, prohibited or limited entry by new firms, subsidized certain consumers at the expense of others, and yet co-existed uncontroversially with relatively free markets (for example, in mining, manufacturing, distribution, and services) in an economy where competition rather than regulation was still presumed to be the norm.

### *The Interstate Commerce Commission*[2]

The American experience with economic regulation began with the Interstate Commerce Act of 1887, which created the Interstate Commerce Commission (ICC) to regulate railroads. The impetus for the act came largely from the railroads themselves. Railroad companies had tried to enact cartel agreements, but their efforts were unsuccessful due to rampant cheating in the form of secret price cuts. The railroads wanted federal regulation to stabilize their cartel. Shippers, the railroads' customers, favored creation of a federal regulator as well. A patchwork of state regulation had led to an ironic situation wherein short hauls often cost shippers more than long hauls.

The Interstate Commerce Act made it illegal to charge more for a short haul than a long haul, but it otherwise represented

---

[2] Marcus Alexis, *The Applied Theory of Regulation: Political Economy at the Interstate Commerce Commission*, 39 Public Choice 5, 6 (1982).

a victory for the railroads. Rates had to be posted publicly and discounts or rebates for individual customers were prohibited. Rates had to be "reasonable," but they were not set by the ICC. A series of amendments cemented the role of the ICC as an enforcer of a railroad cartel that could set minimum and maximum rates, enjoin proposed rates it deemed unreasonable, and control the entry and exit of firms.

When the rise of trucking in the 1920s and 1930s threatened the railroads' dominance in shipping, the railroads sought federal regulation to limit the trucking industry's growth. Incumbent trucking companies, hoping to erect entry barriers, supported regulation as well. The Congress responded in 1935 by extending the ICC's jurisdiction to motor carriers. The agency was given the power to regulate entry and rates in order to limit the supposed dangers of competition. As a result, shippers were captive to ICC-enforced cartels in both modes.

### The Federal Radio Commission[3]

The Radio Act of 1927 was another example of legislation that awarded rents to a powerful industry in the guise of serving the "public interest." During the early years of radio, the Department of Commerce issued broadcasting licenses on a first-come-first-served basis, and broadcasters bought and sold spectrum rights freely. The courts resolved disputes between broadcasters with conflicting signals and the resulting system of property rights worked reasonably well to prevent excessive radio interference.[4] The largest established broadcasters, however, wanted to exclude new entry into their industry. They pushed for the creation of a

---

3   Thomas W. Hazlett, *The Rationality of U.S. Regulation of the Broadcast Spectrum*, 33 J.L. & Econ. 133 (1990).

4   Leonard P. Liggio and Tom G. Palmer, *Freedom and the Law: A Comment on Professor Aranson's Article*, 11 Harv. J.L. & Pol'y 713, 715 (1988).

new federal regulator empowered to limit entry according to "the public interest."

In 1926, a federal court denied the authority of the Department of Commerce to regulate the spectrum. The ensuing confusion provided the justification for Congress to create the Federal Radio Commission (FRC), predecessor of the Federal Communications Commission. The FRC was empowered to award spectrum licenses to whomever it deemed most likely to further "the public interest." The new commission granted incumbent broadcasters exclusive use of the portions of the spectrum they were already using, free of charge. With the support of the broadcasters, it also limited the portion of the spectrum available for commercial radio. The effect was to entrench the most powerful broadcasters, drive out smaller players, and limit entry by newcomers.

### The New Deal

President Franklin D. Roosevelt and his New Deal brought an onslaught of new regulators and regulations, most of them modeled on the ICC. The New Deal was the key intellectual event in the creation of the modern administrative state. Within a few years, agriculture, banking, securities, airlines, and other industries were placed under the control of newly created federal agencies. We had the Securities Act and the Glass-Steagall Banking Act (in 1933), the Securities Exchange Act and the Communications Act (in 1934), the Federal Water Power Act Amendments (in 1935), the Agricultural Adjustment Act and the Civil Aeronautics Act (in 1938), and many more.

The ambition of the New Deal was to regulate the entire economy, as expressed in the National Industrial Recovery Act (NIRA) of 1933. The idea of the NIRA, borrowed from the corporatism of Mussolini, was to manage each industry through a tri-partite council of employers, labor, and government, which would issue so-called "codes of fair competition." In the slogan of the Italian Fascists, *"Tutto nello Stato, niente al di fuori dello Stato, nulla contro lo Stato"* ("Everything for the state, nothing outside the state, nothing against the state"). In the New Deal version, the purpose was, of course, to combat the then rampant price deflation and consequent unemployment: competition would be limited and prices increased in order to enhance producers' revenues, which could then be used to raise wages, thereby increasing purchasing power and demand. In the Schechter Poultry case, a unanimous Supreme Court held this whole scheme unconstitutional because it regulated local rather than interstate commerce and was a wholesale delegation of the legislative power vested in the Congress.

> With the support of the broadcasters, [the Federal Radio Commission] limited the portion of the spectrum available for commercial radio. The effect was to entrench the most powerful broadcasters, drive out smaller players, and limit entry by newcomers.

Unlike the NIRA, the many industry-specific regulatory schemes I mentioned before were upheld. These schemes would go unchallenged during the 1940s and '50s, no doubt bolstered by the prosperity of the post-War era. The national attitude toward economic regulation, if there was one, could be summed up as: "If it ain't broke, don't fix it."

## II. The Pushback against Economic Regulation
Renewed attention to regulatory economics began only in the late 1960s, under the leadership of antitrust scholars—both lawyers such as Richard Posner and micro-economists such as George

Stigler, schooled to believe that *competition* is the best "regulator" of markets. And competition, as you know, maximizes consumer welfare, not producer profits.

These scholars saw that many regulated markets were structurally competitive. That is, they involved a large enough number of firms that there was little reason to fear monopoly pricing, and there was no other obvious rationale for their economic regulation. I refer here to such regulated industries as airlines; motor carriers; railroads, which are few but for much freight compete with trucks, which are numerous; barges; deposit accounts at financial institutions; and natural gas, which was produced by hundreds of field producers.

Another thing that antitrust scholars brought to their inspection of these regulatory regimes was the realization that private firms are rarely able to sustain cartels or otherwise to collude without the aid of government. In fact, it seemed most plausible to explain economic regulation of structurally competitive industries as the device by which government supported industry cartels that otherwise probably could not survive and would, in any event, violate the antitrust laws. Indeed, a little historical research revealed that as with railroads, truckers, and broadcasters, in most cases, industry-specific economic regulatory regimes had been imposed by government at the request of the industry to be regulated!

> **Private firms are rarely able to sustain cartels or otherwise to collude without the aid of government.**

The final irony they found was that the regulated industries did not typically earn monopoly profits under regulation. Instead, they were either bankrupted by inept regulators, as were the railroads, or they were satisfied to live a quiet life, as did the AT&T telephone monopoly, or most commonly, they found loopholes through which to vent their competitive instincts. As some of you may know, there was an era when airlines served creditable meals and featured first-run movies. Indeed during the inflation of the late 1970s, regulation of the interest rates that banks could pay to depositors led them instead to attract deposits by giving away everything from toasters to automobiles.

This revisionist view of economic regulation as something that, far from being vaguely protective of the consuming public, was in fact a front for politically powerful industries to shield themselves (sometimes unsuccessfully) from competition, was academic in origin, had distinctly bipartisan appeal, and proved enormously influential.

## *Airline Deregulation*

Deregulation of the airlines was one of the first successes of this new way of thinking. Commercial aviation had been regulated by the Civil Aeronautics Board (CAB) since 1938. The CAB regulated airfares, limited entry, and even determined which routes would be served by which carriers.

During the 1960s and early '70s, a number of academic empirical studies demonstrated that the CAB's regulations were harming airline consumers.[5] The studies showed rampant inefficiency, and prices much higher than a competitive level.

Senator Ted Kennedy seized on this evidence to push for airline deregulation. In 1975, he hired future Supreme Court Justice Stephen Breyer, then a law professor at Harvard, to lead hearings during which officials from the Antitrust Division, the Federal Trade Commission, the Department of Transportation, the Council of Economic Advisors, and other agencies decried the current system of airline regulation. Consumer advocate Ralph

---

5  Stephen G. Breyer, *Regulation and Its Reform* 317–18(1982) (listing several studies relied upon by the Subcommittee).

Nader called for total deregulation. Support for the status quo came primarily from the airlines and the CAB itself. In the end, the airlines were set free and forced to compete.

Deregulation predictably achieved positive results. New airlines entered the market,[6] prices fell, and air travel was for the first time affordable by everyone.

### *Surface Transportation Deregulation*

The Carter administration's deregulatory efforts did not stop with airlines. In a debate with Ronald Reagan, President Carter boasted: "We have deregulated the air industry, the rail industry, the trucking industry, financial institutions. We're now working on the communications industry."[7] And it was all true.

The 4R Act of 1978 and the Staggers Act of 1980 removed much of the ICC's authority over railroads, quickly producing significant benefits. A trend of increasing prices reversed, costs decreased, industry profits increased, and safety improved.[8] Both the railroads and their customers were better off. The Motor Carrier Act of 1980 loosened the ICC's regulatory authority over trucking, again to the benefit of consumers.[9]

---

6   Id. at 93–94.

7   Matt Welch, *Op-Ed: Democrats These Days Hate Deregulation, But Once Upon a Time They Loved It*, L.A. Times (Feb. 8, 2018).

8   Federal Railroad Administration, *Impact of the Staggers Rail Act of 1980* (Mar. 2011), https://www.fra.dot.gov/Elib/Document/1645; Clifford Winston, The Success of the Staggers Rail Act of 1980 (AEI-Brookings Joint Center for Reg. Studies Paper 05-24, 2005), https://www.brookings.edu/wp-content/uploads/2016/06/10_railact_winston.pdf.

9   Thomas Gale Moore, Rail and Truck Reform: The Record So Far, 7 Regulation 33 (1983).

## Financial Deregulation

Banking was another industry where deregulation was sorely needed during the Carter administration.[10] At the time, interest rates on checking and savings accounts were capped by a regulation dating back to the Glass-Steagall Act of 1933. The caps became a major problem during the "stagflation" of the 1970s, as banks could not offer savers a market rate of return.[11] A 1980 statute created a committee to phase out the interest rate controls. Ironically, one of the committee's first acts was to limit free giveaways—the so-called "toaster rule"[12]—even though the committee was supposed to eliminate the problem that created the need for giveaways.

## The Reagan Administration

When President Reagan took office in 1981, he continued the deregulatory trend, primarily through executive rather than legislative action. One of his first acts in office was to establish a Presidential Task Force on Regulatory Relief.

The Task Force's top priority was relief for the automotive industry, which was being strangled by regulations from the National Highway Traffic Safety Administration (NHTSA) and the Environmental Protection Agency (EPA).[13] Those two agencies now turned to rescinding and relaxing regulations of automakers.

---

10  Matthew Sherman, Ctr. for Econ. Pol'y & Res., *A Short History of Financial Deregulation in the United States* (2009), http://cepr.net/documents/publications/dereg-timeline-2009-07.pdf.

11  Douglas D. Evanoff, Fed. Reserve Bank of Chi., *Assessing the Impact of Regulation on Bank Cost Efficiency*, 22 Econ. Persps. 21 (1998).

12  Stanley M. Gorinson, *Depository Institution Regulatory Reform in the 1980s*, 28 Antitrust Bull. 227, 231 n.10 (1983).

13  Jerry L. Mashaw and David L. Harfst, *From Command and Control to Collaboration and Deference: The Transformation of Auto Safety Regulation*, 34 Yale J. Reg. 167, 188 (2017).

> **Even now, more resources are commandeered and reallocated by federal regulation than by taxing and spending.**

President Reagan also issued an Executive Order that, for the first time, required agencies, before issuing a new regulation, to submit a cost-benefit analysis for approval by the White House Office of Management and Budget. This important innovation, in place ever since, was the first step towards rationalizing the rulemaking process. Even now, more resources are commandeered and reallocated by federal regulation than by taxing and spending. Any president who wants to see his policies implemented must control what the regulatory state does.

### Global Reach of Deregulation[14]
Following the lead of the United States, the United Kingdom deregulated coal, steel, railroads, telecommunications, and utilities under Margaret Thatcher's government in the 1980s. Chile, also influenced by the United States and by Chicago economists in particular, deregulated large swaths of its economy and privatized the pension scheme during this same period. Emboldened by these countries' success, other European and Latin American countries followed suit, to varying degrees, during the 1990s. Unfortunately, the story does not end there.

### III. The Rise of Risk Regulation
As economic regulation was diminishing in the United States, risk regulation was exploding. Risk regulation, unlike the economic regulation that began with the railroads, does not impose direct limits on competition. Whereas economic regulation seeks to control entry and pricing in an industry, risk regulation seeks

---
14   World Bank, *Economic Growth in the 1990s: Learning from a Decade of Reform* 165–67(2005).

to limit the risks an industry imposes on others, most often due to real or imagined market failures. For example, a factory may find it rational to pollute the air because the harms it causes are born by others; the lack of property rights in the air creates a true market failure. Regulators may properly respond to this externality problem by setting limits on the volume of emission and thereby requiring pollution control equipment, and/or granting tradeable pollution permits. When done correctly, risk regulation is a net benefit to society. All too often, however, it has inefficient results and it always has unintended and unwanted consequences.

Risk regulation proliferated in the United States during the 1970s. In the space of ten years, Congress passed the Clean Air Act, the Clean Water Act, the Consumer Product Safety Act, the Highway Safety Act, the Occupational Health and Safety Act, the Federal Mine Safety and Health Act, and more.

Other countries adopted similar forms of risk regulation as they attained similar levels of prosperity. The European Union adopted its first environmental policy in 1973, whereas China began its environmental regulatory program only in 2013.[15] Today, the EU's environmental policy is characterized by the excessive risk aversion of the so-called "precautionary principle," which mandates that regulators err on the side of more regulation whenever there is uncertainty[16]—and there is always uncertainty in the science relevant to risks.

---

15   Christian Hey, *EU Environmental Policies: A Short History of the Policy Strategies*, https://pdfs.semanticscholar.org/445e/f8210932ca2b848b8d8b0d46072b592d97ae.pdf; Yangzhong Huang, *Why China's Good Environmental Policies Have Gone Wrong*, N.Y. Times: Opinion (2018), https://www.nytimes.com/2018/01/14/opinion/china-environmental-policies-wrong.html (China's environmental efforts started in 2013).

16   *Future Brief: The Precautionary Principle: Decision-making Under Uncertainty, European Commission* (2017), https://ec.europa.eu/environment/integration/research/newsalert/pdf/precautionary_principle_decision_making_under_uncertainty_FB18_en.pdf; *The Development of EU Environmental Law*, http://www2.balticuniv.uu.se/bup-3/index.php/public/textbooks-course-materials/course-materials/sustainable-development-course/chapter-9/1367-em1-chapter-2-development-of-eu-environmental-regulation.

Risk regulation laws respond to real, not imagined hazards—such as pollution, traffic fatalities, and worker injuries—but the question remains whether some of these hazards would respond better to market forces. For example, the labor market gives employers an incentive to mitigate known workplace safety hazards because workers demand higher wages to compensate for hazards of which they are aware.[17] Studies suggest workers are generally well-informed about the accident risks incident to working in their industry.[18] Health hazards, such as the likelihood of developing a disease due to long-term chemical exposure, will usually be less obvious to workers. It follows that workplace regulators, such as the OSHA, should address primarily latent health risks and leave to the marketplace accident risks that are apparent to workers.

For hazards that do not respond to market forces, the question is how best to design a regulatory scheme to minimize the cost of achieving the desired level of safety. Take environmental regulation. A regulator could control pollution by setting a maximum level of emissions for each source or by mandating the use of certain environmentally friendly technologies. As the Nobel Laureate Ronald Coase taught us, however, the source of the environmental pollution problem is the absence of property rights. A better way to solve the pollution problem, therefore, is to auction tradeable pollution permits that grant a property right in emissions. This allows the market to arrive at an efficient solution—assuming the regulator has correctly estimated the amount of pollution that is optimal. Many jurisdictions, including China, California, and the European Union, and the U.S. have

---

17   W. Kip Viscusi et al., *Economics of Regulation and Antitrust* 831 (2005).

18   W. Kip Viscusi & Charles O'Connor, *Adaptive Responses to Chemical Labeling: Are Workers Bayesian Decisionmakers?*, 74 American Economic Review 942–56 (1984); W. Kip Viscusi, *Employment Hazards: An Investigation of Market Performance* (1979).

selectively instituted market-based "cap-and-trade" solutions to reduce carbon emissions.[19]

A market-based solution similar to cap-and-trade has succeeded in combatting the depletion of several fisheries. If fisheries are not subjected to any regulation at all, fisherman have an incentive to capture as many fish as possible without regard to the long-term health of the fishery—a classic tragedy of the commons scenario.[20]

Early attempts at regulation required each fishing vessel to get a license, and set the Total Allowable Catch for the fishery as a whole. Naturally, the captains raced to catch as many fish as possible early in the season. This "race for fish" was highly inefficient, as fishermen over-invested in technologies that allowed them to catch more fish. The initial regulatory response was to establish monthly limits on the number of trips by each vessel. The trip limits did not eliminate the race, however. Instead, they encouraged fishermen to catch more fish per trip. Eventually the season had to be limited to one day per year.

Enter Individual Transferable Quotas (ITQs), which grant individual fishermen a property right in a certain share of the Total Allowable Catch. If the ITQ is freely tradeable and of unlimited duration, then the fishermen's incentives are aligned with the long-term health of the fishery. This encourages the use of more efficient practices and discourages the industry from lobbying regulators to raise the total catch above the sustainable level. Empirical studies suggest that when an ITQ regime is put into place, fish populations recover, and fishermen enjoy larger catches.[21] It is no wonder, then, that the ITQ approach has steadily gained traction since the 1980s.

---

19   *How Cap and Trade Works, Environmental Defense Fund*, https://www.edf.org/climate/how-cap-and-trade-works.

20   Nowlis and Bentham, *Do Property Rights Lead to Sustainable Catch Increases?*, 27 Marine Resource Economics 89, 91 (2012).

21   Christopher Costello et al., *Can Catch Shares Prevent Fisheries Collapse?*, 321 *Science* 1678 (2008); Heal & Schlenker, Sustainable Fisheries, 455 Nature 1044 (2008).

## IV. Conclusion

The point of this talk has been to remind you of the important lessons of the twentieth century, lest we forget them in the twenty-first.

The economic deregulation of the 1970s and '80s was extremely successful, yet today, some would bring us back to the New Deal era. Presidential candidates vow to regulate drug prices[22] and impose rent controls on apartments.[23] The White House is reportedly considering further intervention to boost the struggling coal industry, which faces likely fatal competition from cheap natural gas.[24] There have been calls to regulate the internet from every angle, from net neutrality—a cleverly named price control regime—to a proposed ban on vertical integration by digital platform companies,[25] to a bill to limit users' time on Twitter to thirty minutes per day.[26] A newly passed California law, motivated primarily by Uber and the so-called "gig economy," will reclassify many independent contractors as employees, and set strict limits on freelancing in many industries (not just online platforms).[27] Under this law, freelance journalists will be limited to publishing 35 articles per site each year, in the vain hope that media out-

---

[22] Elizabeth Warren's *Ambitious New Bill to Lower Generic Drug Prices, Explained*, Vox (Dec. 20, 2018), https://www.vox.com/policy-and-politics/2018/12/20/18146993/elizabeth-warren-2020-election-drug-prices-bill

[23] *Housing for All*, Bernie Sanders, https://berniesanders.com/issues/housing-all/ ("We need to establish a national rent control standard").

[24] *Trump Can't Save Coal Country*, Foreign Policy (Oct. 30, 2019), https://foreignpolicy.com/2019/10/30/trump-save-coal-country-murray-bankruptcy-gas/.

[25] *Elizabeth Warren, Here's How We Can Break up Big Tech, Medium* (Mar. 8, 2019), https://medium.com/@teamwarren/heres-how-we-can-break-up-big-tech-9ad9e-0da324c; Elizabeth Warren on Breaking up Amazon: 'You Don't Get to be the Umpire and Have a Team', Huffington Post (Apr. 23, 2019), https://www.huffpost.com/entry/elizabeth-warren-tech-amazon_n_5cbe6120e4b00b3e70ce32b8.

[26] *Josh Hawley's bill to limit your Twitter time to 30 minutes a day*, RECODE (July 31, 2019), https://www.vox.com/recode/2019/7/31/20748732/josh-hawley-smart-act-social-media-addiction.

[27] *California Destroys $1 Trillion Gig Economy with New Law*, Forbes (Oct. 31, 2019), https://www.forbes.com/sites/heidilynnekurter/2019/10/31/california-destroys-1-trillion-gig-economy-with-new-law/#7b7c328e2f0d.

lets will therefore hire more of them as staff writers—a scheme guaranteed to have perverse consequences. These interventions in the functioning of markets are sure to have adverse effects, just as New Deal-era economic regulation did.

The second takeaway from the twentieth century is the mixed success of risk regulation. Environmental regulations are most effective when they rely upon market mechanisms. Moving forward, legislatures and regulators would be wise to avoid command-and-control approaches to environmental sustainability and embrace the creation of property rights. The Green New Deal advocated by some self-styled "Progressives" in Congress would ignore this lesson, instead mandating the use of particular technologies, such as high-speed rail and renewable energy sources.[28] It would also use economic regulation, protectionist trade policies, and the antitrust laws indirectly to lower carbon emissions.[29]

Moving forward, these and other proposed economic regulations should be treated with extreme skepticism. Existing economic regulations should be studied, as the airline regulations were and, if they are found to be harmful, rescinded, not replicated. Risk regulations should be designed in a manner that preserves competition to the extent possible, preferably by assigning property rights and allowing market mechanisms to decrease risks in the most efficient way.

As Winston Churchill said, "Those who fail to learn from history are condemned to repeat it." The history of regulation is no exception.

---

28   *Resolution Recognizing the Duty of the Federal Government to Create a Green New Deal*, H.R. Res. 109, 116th Cong. (Feb. 7, 2019), https://www.congress.gov/116/bills/hres109/BILLS-116hres109ih.pdf.

29   29 Id. at pp. 8, 13–14.

7

# CONTEXT, CONTINUITY, AND TRUTH: THEORY, HISTORY, AND POLITICAL ECONOMY

*By Peter Boettke*

---

Peter Boettke was serving a two-year term as president of the Mont Pelerin Society, in addition to his role as university professor of economics and philosophy at George Mason University, when he gave his Liggio Lecture in New York City on November 8, 2017, as part of Atlas Network's Liberty Forum. He acknowledged helpful comments from Rosolino Candela, Chris Coyne, and Peter Leeson in preparation of his Liggio Lecture.

The lecture itself explores the stewardship responsibility of classical liberals to provide a robust defense of our vision of a society of free and responsible individuals. Peter highlights the threat posed by critical theorists who advance narratives instead of seeking truth and who tempt liberals down the same path.

---

It is a great honor for me to give the Liggio Lecture here at Atlas Network's Liberty Forum. Leonard Liggio truly was the Ambassador of Liberty throughout his amazing career. He was also a great friend and mentor to many of us in this room. My first interactions with Leonard were through the Institute for Humane Studies in the early 1980s; he was a teacher and a mentor. My last interactions with Leonard were through our work together with the Fund for the Study of Spontaneous Order in the 2000s and 2010s.

In between, Leonard became a constant source of encouragement in my career, source of ideas of interest to pursue, and source of connections to develop within the network of scholars as a graduate student and then as a faculty member. At my first job, Leonard arranged for the Liberty Fund catalogue of books to be donated to my university library.

Leonard pushed me to submit my work to be considered for awards, such as the Hayek Prize from Mont Pelerin Society, and he also championed my membership with MPS early in my career—and now I am president of that organization. Leonard arranged to get me invited to Liberty Fund conferences, and even to be hired by Liberty Fund to consult on a project to reinvigorate the economic wing of their conference and publishing program. Leonard also encouraged me to attend the History of Economic Society meetings, as well as the American Economic Association, the Association for Private Enterprise Education, the Public Choice Society, and the Southern Economic Association. Leonard argued that professional engagement for scholarship and network building was important to one's career. He celebrated my faculty appointments at NYU and then at GMU, and he convinced me to apply to be part of Templeton's Freedom Project.

As you can tell, Leonard's support, encouragement, and intellectual example was indispensable in my own development as an academic economist. Leonard always exhibited deep, not surface-level, learning across disciplines, but especially in history and intellectual history—so scholarship. Leonard always exhibited respect for others, not strategic manipulation, and mutual respect in the community of learners—so Left and Right. And, finally, Leonard, while always curious and always respectful, was also firmly planted in the sciences of human action—so Mises and praxeology. And by praxeology, Leonard meant not a restrictive methodological/epistemological stance but instead the application of the methods associated with the economic way of thinking beyond the study of the market process to all walks of human actions and interaction.

Leonard tells us in his biographical notes that when he first came to study with Mises after reading *Human Action* upon its publication in 1949, the Mises seminar was devoted at that time to his presentation of the materials that would become *Theory and History* (1957). This is important because Leonard was studying history and engaged in the literature of European political, legal, and economic history, as well as the intellectual history of classical liberalism, in particular the French liberal tradition of Jean-Baptiste Say and Frédéric Bastiat. In short, it is always important to remember that as a scholar, Leonard was both a historian and a historian of ideas, and he weaved between these seamlessly to address liberty and power from the Middle Ages to the twentieth century.[1]

So, on this occasion I believe it is appropriate to take a moment to acknowledge Leonard Liggio's life of scholarship, teaching, mentorship, and institutional entrepreneurship. Leonard identified, encouraged, connected, and created opportunities for many of us in this room, and without his presence in our lives we very well may not be here right now. We all owe him so much.

And for my talk, I hope to suggest one way we can repay that intellectual debt. The most obvious is to be a good steward to the intellectual tradition of classical liberalism. The great Frédéric Bastiat once wrote that we should never fear an artful critique of our position, but always fear an inept defense. It is our responsibility to be the best scholars and teachers of classical liberal political econ-

> **The great Frédéric Bastiat once wrote that we should never fear an artful critique of our position, but always fear an inept defense.**

---

[1] See the three-part biographical sketch on Leonard at the Liggio Project—https://leonardliggio.org/?page_id=221

## Context, Continuity, and Truth: Theory, History, and Political Economy

omy that we can be—to think clearly, speak clearly, and write clearly, and to tackle tough questions and take on, in the most rigorous and sophisticated way possible, the popular fallacies of our age that tend to cut against the argument for a society of free and responsible individuals.

With this task in mind, what I want to talk about today is the dilemma of our day in carrying out that task. There is, I contend, an intellectual crisis in both the fields of intellectual history and in the discipline of history more generally. It is a crisis regarding the status of truth-seeking in the disciplines. A new generation of critical theorists are seeking to poke holes in the history of economic theory and liberal political economy, and to demonstrate the inherent inefficiency, instability, and immorality of the capitalist system. And just to hopefully ignite some stimulating conversation, I am going to suggest that economic approaches that are not rooted in the Misesian and Hayekian economic way of thinking that Leonard championed are decidedly ill-equipped to face these new challenges. Instead, they lead to the abandoning of the disciplines of history and intellectual history. And, if we economists abandon history—in both senses—we leave our past to the kindness of our enemies.[2] This is an extremely vulnerable position to find oneself in. Yet this is where we are. Leonard would want us to correct that, so let's do that.

---

2  I owe the recognition of this basic dilemma that economists face to my colleague David Levy. A classic example of this is told in Levy's "How the Dismal Science Got Its Name" (2002). Most commentaries uninformed about the economic content of the disputes of the time believe the name derives from some Malthusian observation or the disciplinary insistence on scarcity and constraints, but Thomas Carlyle and his literary cohort was attacking classical economists for their analytical egalitarianism and their refusal to accept a natural hierarchy of mankind. It was the classical economists, Levy documents, that opposed the institution of slavery, as well as argued that the Irish were not inherently inferior to the English. Thus, if economists abandon our history, we let others read back into the past the discourse that they are most familiar with and that fits most comfortably into their ideological priors. They are either unaware or unwilling to tackle the arguments that were actually made by economists in the time being discussed.

What is truth in the social sciences and humanities? During the 1970s and 1980s, as the positivist philosophical program came under increasing scrutiny, among the post-positivist positions articulated was post-modernism, and among post-modernists were critical theorists and deconstructivists.

It is one thing to claim that social scientists cannot hermetically seal themselves off from ethical values and various biases and pursue purely objective analysis, but it is quite another thing to claim that this means that the entire enterprise of "objective" analysis is a sham. To say knowledge of the social world—and knowledge of our efforts to understand the social world—is embedded in an intricate matrix of values, social meanings, and contextualization does not imply that there are no basic facts of the situation, or that there are no ways to adjudicate between competing explanations or theoretical frameworks. Of course, facts do not speak for themselves, and thus all knowledge of the social world demands contextualization and recognition of its social construction. But also not all interpretations of events are equally as grounded, and not all arguments are equally valid. Progress in the social sciences and humanities can be made.

> **Most economists are trained to avoid such murky epistemological waters, but even in their practice they don't. Rather, they just avoid recognizing that they are drowning in them.**

Most economists are trained to avoid such murky epistemological waters, but even in their practice they don't. Rather, they just avoid recognizing that they are drowning in them. To say that if something is important we must measure it, bleeds too quickly into the claim that whatever we can measure, we should claim as being important. It is not! Now is not the time to discuss in any detail the various shortcomings of the empirical project in the social sciences, except to note that the substitution of sophisticated statistical analysis for more narrative history does not solve the problems that have plagued social science and history since their very beginning. The only way to "solve" them is to recognize them and embrace multiple forms of evidence and multiple methods of analysis. But many economic historians argue that this is precisely not the way to solve the problem. Instead, they insist we must just count—count correctly and thoroughly. But let me be clear that nobody should be against counting. In fact, counting can fix a lot of confusion in social sciences and history. When Hayek edited *Capitalism and the Historians*, basic counting was used to challenge the prevailing opinions about the immiseration of the working class during the Industrial Revolution. And more recently, Deirdre McCloskey stresses in her history of the Great Enrichment that you cannot answer empirical questions philosophically, so we have to count when doing responsible history. But she is still doing history.

In a recent paper, Robert Margo (2017) explored the progress economic historians have made over the last generation within the economics profession. How he measured progress, however, was whether economic historians looked in their work more and more like economists and less like historians. In other words, if you pick up an article in the *Journal of Economic History* (JEH) and compare it to the *Journal of Political Economy* (JPE), what do you see in terms of words, formulas, tables, and charts? By Margo's measure, what has happened over the past twenty years is that the form and substance of articles in the JEH and the JPE have become increasingly indistinguishable from each other. Economists count, and economic historians count, they don't read so much as they once did, they don't contextualize as was once expected, and they certainly don't look for meanings associated with the human condition historically contemplated. Economic historians in essence have ceded history to the historians; they do economics but by counting and calculating with data from the deeper past, rather than the more recent past or the present. But let's not get confused. These economic historians are economists, and thus they approach their research and produce results that look the same as their fellow economists. Margo tells us not to fear, though, since economists have better employment opportunities and higher compensation. He is, of course, right on this last point. But what happens if economic historians abandon history?

We already know the answer—we get new histories of capitalism, which focus on exploitation of man, monopoly power, alienation, and periodic crises. Capitalism is plagued by inefficiency, suffers instability, and is characterized by injustice. Effectively addressing these arguments requires more than counting. It might be important here to remember that there is a world of difference between being heard and being listened to, so in the exchange between historians of capitalism and economic historians of capitalism, insisting on counting by the economists while ignoring all the other issues—including the problems with power, politics, culture, and the long shadow of past imperfections—means one might be heard but not listened to, and moving the intellectual climate of opinion requires earning such a hearing. Counting, in other words, is a necessary component to the explanation of capitalism but is not sufficient.

**What happens if economic historians abandon history?**

History is more than counting. It requires contextualization and comparative analysis, and to do that, sound economic theory is critical. Enter once again Mises's *Theory and History* (1957)—economists need to be economists, not mathematicians and statisticians, in order to do economic history. The problem with the contemporary histories of capitalism is weak theory more so than innumeracy, though innumeracy doesn't help. Too many historians of capitalism are arguing that the legacy of slavery and colonization benefited the West and not trade, technological innovation, and entrepreneurial creativity. They see the world in negative sum terms, they misunderstand the institutional preconditions for realizing productive specialization and peaceful social cooperation among diverse and often distant people. In short, they have a bad theory of economic development and the role that a private property market economy plays in that process of material progress. Deirdre McCloskey refers to economic development as "trade-tested betterment," and much of the modern history of capitalism is allergic to this way of thinking about it. History is too important to be left to the "historians." I am arguing that this bad intellectual state of history is a consequence of economists abandoning economic history and the intellectual history of classical and modern political economy and economics to their intellectual enemies.

But the problem that must be addressed isn't limited to bad history. The intellectual history of economics is also experiencing its own crisis. Reading the history of economic theory can be divided into at least three broad approaches: (1) internal logic of arguments in texts, (2) ideas in context, and (3) hermeneutics of suspicion. There are other fine distinctions that can be introduced such as Whig, contra-Whig, antiquarian, and instrumental (see Boettke 2000). The classic task for economists from prior to Adam Smith until the post-WWII era was for economists to engage in close textual readings of arguments and to assess the strengths and weaknesses of different arguments on their own internal consistencies, the comparative analysis with other arguments, and the correspondence with the issues in the world which the theories were being developed to address. Economics evolved during its first 150 years as a philosophical subject. During the past seventy years, economics has shifted from being a philosophical science to becoming a mathematical and statistical science. The transformation of economics can actually be traced to the turn of the twentieth century, but it was not completely accomplished until after WWII—as prior to that the more philosophical thinkers existed side-by-side with the more scientific thinkers in the elite corners of the profession. Amartya Sen argued in *On Ethics and Economics* (1987) that economics as a discipline exists on an intellectual production possibility frontier between economics as a moral science and economics as social engineering. Since he was interested in reintroducing ethical discourse back into economics, Sen argued that the economics profession was operating in the corner solution of social engineering and it was time for the profession to trade-off and move back toward moral sciences. Of course, he doesn't advocate a corner solution in that direction either, but just significant movement back toward political economy and social philosophy.

Studying the shifting intellectual landscape of economics is the task of historians of economics. The exercise of intellectual history in political economy and economics improved when close textual reading was complimented by contextualization in the same way that political theory was contextualized with the Cambridge School of intellectual history: our understanding of the evolution of ideas improved. Scholars and scientists do not work in a vacuum, but instead always within an intellectual, organizational, social, and cultural context. Ideas are not necessarily context dependent, but the way ideas are communicated, which ideas coalesce into a consensus, and which ones get cast aside are context dependent. This is why the evolution of ideas is never smooth but always full of fascinating twists and turns defined by missteps, wrong turns, and the continual re-evaluation of arguments. Thus, the potency of the contra-Whig position in intellectual history. The Whig tradition of intellectual history basically argues that all that is good in the ancients is embodied already in the moderns, so there really is not much value besides antiquarian tastes in reading Adam Smith or David Ricardo or John Stuart Mill.[3] But what if due to the misallocation of intellectual resources that results from fads and fashions in science, there are ideas from the past that have not exhausted their evolutionary potential? If this is the case, then ideas from an older thinker can remain part of our extended present, and could in fact be a vital input into contemporary theory construction.

As economists, this disruptive and disjointed evolution of ideas becomes even more fascinating when we place ourselves in the model of intellectual development itself. The economics of economics, or more broadly the sociology of science, matters. In one sense, it is a natural outgrowth of putting ideas in context, but in another way, it opens up another avenue of research and exploration. We can study the incentive structures of science and scholarship, including how professional activities in any discipline are organized. Funding, positions, and prestige must be addressed alongside of the assessment of ideas and their application to the world of affairs. Again, our understanding of the process of scientific advancement is improved when we explore the "organization of inquiry." But here is a critical point to remember about an economics of economics: to be effective it has to be grounded in sound economic theory. Sound economics doesn't focus our attention on matters of personal psychology and strict adherence to preference and motivation

---

[3] The classic statement of Whig history of economic thought is George Stigler (1969) in "Does Economics Have a Useful Past?" In 1976, McCloskey asked, "Does the Past Have Useful Economics?" Part of my purpose here is to recommend that our contemporary situation demands that we re-examine these questions and re-engage the interrelationship between theory and history in our study of the past and the present.

based explanations. Instead, the focus of attention is on the systemic incentives that alternative institutional arrangements produce in commercial and non-commercial life, including science and scholarship. In an analysis so pursued, the advancement of science and the tracking of truth does not depend on the individual motives of those involved, but on the institutional incentives and the ability of the organization of inquiry to produce a constructive conversation in which views are subject to continual contestation.

> **The critical point to take away from economics is that its explanatory thrust is to be found in institutional variation, not in behavioral differences among people.**

The honorable tradition of liberal political economy sought first and foremost to explore the technical principles necessary to understand how alternative institutional arrangements impact our ability to realize productive specialization and peaceful social cooperation. In developing this line of thinking, political economists adopted a sort of analytical egalitarianism—a basic behavioral symmetry. People are people, my Mom used to say, but so did my teachers James Buchanan and Gordon Tullock. Same players, different rules, results in different games.[4] The critical point to take away from economics is that its explanatory thrust is to be found in institutional variation, not in behavioral differences among people. Methodologically and analytically, the question then becomes how best to study institutional variation.

---

[4] See the first chapter in the public choice primer *Government Failure: A Primer on Public Choice* written by Tullock and republished in 2005. Chapter one is titled "People are People: Elements of Public Choice Theory." Also see Buchanan's "Same Players, Different Game: How Better Rules Makes Better Politics" (2008).

But isn't it easier to focus on behavioral differences? Bad people do bad things. Stupid people do stupid things. So we want to avoid bad and stupid people, and trust in good and smart people. Such a perspective is problematic on many levels. But for our purposes here let's state that once we move away from institutional variation and instead look for our explanations in differences among people, we invite a caricature of individuals that we sort into (a) those who are stupid, (b) those who are evil, and (c) those good and smart people who agree with me. Such a division doesn't result in learning, and when taken to its limits destroys the trust among scholars in the quest for human understanding.

The real problem with preference-based explanations of intellectual history as opposed to close textual exegesis and the attempt to place ideas in their historical, philosophical, cultural context, is that personal psychology of ideas comes to be stressed rather than an assessment of arguments and adjudication of evidence for positions. Not only is personal psychology stressed, judgment is passed on the motives inferred (often never proven as this is often impossible to do). So the hermeneutics of suspicion questions not arguments and evidence. And, in much of the literature on neoliberalism, such as the work on Milton Friedman, F. A. Hayek, James Buchanan, and the legacy of MPS, the logic of their arguments is ignored, the empirical evidence related to their arguments is unexamined, but the supposed financial motivations and "will to power" takes center stage and intellectual positions are tied to remote political realities such as Chile, or the global financial crisis.

This is our current intellectual climate. The history of capitalism by historians has resurrected arguments that were effectively challenged from Hayek's *Capitalism and the Historians* to Nathan Rosenberg and L. E. Birdzell's *How the West Grew Rich*, and of course the monumental trilogy by Deirdre McCloskey on *The*

*Bourgeois Era.* And, the history of neoliberal thought and economics in general suggests that these theories and approaches didn't emerge in *The Clash of Economic Ideas,* as my colleague Larry White so brilliantly demonstrates, but instead through manipulation of the scientific process through unjustified positions of power in intellectual affairs obtained through the unwarranted intrusion of funding sources that have corrupted science. *The Merchants of Doubt* (2011) style of argument isn't limited to nuclear power, tobacco, and climate change, but now spreads to the new learning in Chicago Price Theory and Industrial Organization, monetarism and macroeconomic policy, public choice and constitutional political economy, and Austrian economics and libertarianism. *The House of Cards* conspiratorial style of "story telling" about intellectual history identifies "evil geniuses" who devise "master plans" and find the funding from "dark money." Along the way they have not only absconded with prestigious academic positions that are well funded and led to Nobel Prizes, but they have also ruined national economies and destroyed the hopes and dreams of the average individual, not to mention the oppression of their opponents.

These works, whether we are talking about Philip Mirowski or Avner Offer or Nancy MacLean, are easy reading. The story flows easily from their pen. They are entertaining narratives about the intellectual world in the same way seeing Frank Underwood manipulate the politics of D.C. to rise to the presidency is entertaining. But just as *House of Cards* does not portray politics correctly—it is not a public choice analysis of democratic processes—these critiques of the neoliberal thought collective fall short of accuracy. As my good friend Michael Munger (2008, 2015) said of one of these works, it exalts "truthiness" over truth. Among a certain group of progressive intellectuals who have been challenged by the developments in economic theory associated with the Austrian, Chicago, UCLA, and Virginia schools that effectively poked holes in the Keynesian consensus in the decades following WWII with a rejuvenated microeconomics to challenge the hegemony of macroeconomics, and the innovative development of property rights economics, public choice economics, law-and-economics, market process economics, the ability to dismiss rather than having to provide counter arguments was (is) just too attractive. If they can discredit and delegitimize arguments, why would they need to address them? Again, Frank Underwood has no legitimate claim to the office, right?

But rather than end on a note of scolding those I disagree with about the intellectual descent into the hermeneutics of suspicion, I want to warn us—classical liberal scholars and intellectuals—about falling into a similar path. There is an allure, after all, to those ideological blinders. A key to Leonard Liggio's approach to history and intellectual history was no doubt the story of liberty versus power, but Leonard didn't take the easy way out. He didn't argue that the economics profession, for example, was plagued by corruption and confusion due to major funding by those in political power. Austrian economics faced barriers, but Leonard Liggio's argument was to aspiring professors: face those barriers head on and just do better work—work that others in the profession will have to pay attention to, and work that tracks truth. Never settle for comfortable "truthiness" that fits with your ideological priors. So yes, we should acknowledge that when we put economics in the model of economics itself, it does matter in terms of the structure of incentives within the organization of inquiry. But that doesn't exhaust the narrative we tell; it is just one component. Our primary focus begins with the most charitable interpretation of arguments, a close and critical examination of the arguments, and a careful weighing of the evidence.

As I said, Leonard taught us all to be better and to stress scholarship, to find common ground with other scholars left and right, and to practice praxeology to the high standard set by Mises, Hayek, Kirzner, etc., in our quest to understand the human condition. To do that we must recognize the tragedy that results when ideological blinders block scholarship and our continual learning. Let's live up to the standard Leonard set as a life-long learner, and follow his lead in how he encouraged us to pursue and produce scholarship of impact, be teachers that excite, and be mentors that connect to a growing intellectual network.

> **Face those barriers head on and just do better work—work that others in the profession will have to pay attention to, and work that tracks truth. Never settle for comfortable 'truthiness' that fits with your ideological priors.**

## References

Beckert, S. 2015. *Empire of Cotton.* New York, NY: Vintage.

Birdzell, L. E. and Nathan Rosenberg 1987. *How the West Grew Rich.* New York, NY: Basic Books.

Boettke, P. 2000. "Why Read the Classics?" Library of Economics and Liberty (February 24), http://www.econlib.org/library/Features/feature2.html.

Buchanan, J. 2008. "Same Players, Different Games: How Better Rules Makes Better Politics," Constitutional Political Economy 19 (3): 171-179.

Hayek, F. A., ed. 1954. *Capitalism and the Historians.* Chicago, IL: University of Chicago Press.

Levy, D. 2002. *How the Dismal Science Got Its Name.* Ann Arbor, MI: University of Michigan Press.

MacLean, N. 2017. *Democracy in Chains.* New York, NY: Vintage.

McCloskey, D. 1976. "Does the Past Have a Useful Economics?" Journal of Economic Literature 14 (2) 434-461.

McCloskey, D. 2006. *Bourgeois Virtues.* Chicago, IL: University of Chicago Press.

McCloskey, D. 2010. *Bourgeois Dignity.* Chicago, IL: University of Chicago Press.

McCloskey, D. 2016. *Bourgeois Equality.* Chicago, IL: University of Chicago Press.

Mises, L. 1957. *Theory and History.* New Haven, CT: Yale University Press.

Mirowski, P. and Dieter Plehwe, ed. 2009. *The Road to Mont Pelerin.* Cambridge, Mass.: Harvard University Press.

Munger, M. 2008. "Blogging and Political Information," Public Choice 134 (1/2): 125-138.

Munger, M. 2015. "L'Affaire LaCour: What It Can Teach Us About Academic Integrity and Truthiness," Chronicle of Higher

Education (June 15): http://www.chronicle.com/article/LAffaire-LaCour/230905/.

Offer, A. and G. Soderberg. 2016. *The Nobel Factor*. Princeton, NJ: Princeton University Press.

Oreskes, Naomi and Erik Conway. 2011. *Merchants of Doubt*. New York, NY: Bloomsbury Press.

Sen, A. 1987. *On Ethics and Economics*. New York, NY: Wiley.

Stigler, G. 1969. "Does Economics Have a Useful Past?," History of Political Economy 1 (2): 217-230.

Tullock, G., et. al., 2005. *Government Failure: A Primer on Public Choice*. Washington, DC: Cato Institute.

White, L. 2012. *The Clash of Economic Ideas*. New York, NY: Cambridge University Press.

8

# ONCE MORE: LIBERALISM AND SOME PROBLEMS OF HISTORICAL TRANSMISSION BETWEEN THE GENERATIONS

*By Lenore T. Ealy*

---

The ninth Liggio Lecture was delivered at Atlas Network's 2022 Liberty Forum in Miami on December 14, 2022, by Lenore T. Ealy, who had then recently joined Universidad Francisco Marroquín in Guatemala as its vice president international. She was introduced to the Liberty Forum audience by former Atlas Network board chair Linda Whetstone—Linda's last appearance on stage, as she passed away the next day.

In Lenore's Liggio Lecture, she challenges key lines from F.A. Hayek's "The Intellectuals and Socialism," contending (contra Hayek) we classical liberals need to summon the courage NOT to be Utopian. She provides a sweeping look at how we might save younger generations from the socialists' false promises of redemption, asserting it is "more likely to happen in community than in the trenches of political warfare."

---

> "We must make the building of a free society once more an intellectual adventure, a deed of courage."
> —F. A. Hayek
> "The Intellectuals and Socialism" (1949)

Thank you, Linda. It is a great honor for me to be introduced by you, especially because I just heard your presidential address at the Mont Pelerin Society meeting in Guatemala, in which you recited the same familiar lines from Hayek's essay "The Intellectuals and Socialism" that inspired my title for this talk.

## Once More: Liberalism and Some Problems of Historical Transmission between the Generations

I also want to express my thanks to Brad Lips and the Atlas Network team for inviting me to address this audience as the ninth presenter of the annual Liggio Memorial Lecture. It is an honor to join my predecessors in remembering our friend and mentor Leonard Liggio.

If I looked to Hayek for the title of my remarks, it has been Leonard's historical and legal scholarship, his mentoring of countless scholars and political activists over the years, and his kind and pacific personality that have inspired the themes of my remarks.

> **We must do more to understand how we best transmit to future generations not only our ideas but also the desire to participate in a living tradition of classical entrepreneurial liberalism.**

I first met Leonard when I arrived at the Institute for Humane Studies as a summer research fellow in 1990, and Leonard was on hand as a mentor to the eight of us in residence that summer. In the following years I would participate in two of the remarkable summer history seminars organized by Leonard, where I encountered new ideas and forged life-long intellectual friendships. In 1993 I enjoyed participating with Leonard—as well as with my dissertation advisor, John Pocock—in a semester-long seminar at the Folger Library. Later, I would have the pleasure of working with Leonard through the board of The Philadelphia Society and, after he came to Atlas Network, as part of Dick Cornuelle's "kitchen-cabinet." But more on that in a moment.

This morning, I want to share with you some questions that have been on my mind about the relationships between liberalism and democracy, about the transmission of liberalism within the complex tapestry of historical experience, and about the roles of philanthropy and entrepreneurship in the evolution of social institutions.

The success of liberalism depends on doing more than merely once more getting our philosophical ideas right. We must also do more to understand how we best transmit to future generations not only our ideas but also the desire to participate in a living tradition of classical entrepreneurial liberalism.

So, what is the liberal orientation to being in the world and how do we generate, sustain, and renew the liberal tradition?

The liberal worldview rests on respect for the dignity of people and their capability to take responsibility for their own lives, despite the challenges of the human condition. It also calls us to intellectual humility, respecting the limitations of human nature. Recognizing the necessity of social cooperation, liberal systems of self-governance (which we too often equate with "democracy") require us to place additional constraints upon ourselves. Such formal constraints may be born in revelation (such as the "thou shalt nots" of the biblical decalogue) or custom (as by the common law adjudication of disputes) or through legal theory (as in the philosophical principle of non-aggression). We may fix them in laws and constitutions, but as Alexis de Tocqueville observed, the principles and practices that sustain liberty are only realized in history when they become the "habits of the heart" of a people.

> **We may fix them in laws and constitutions, but as Alexis de Tocqueville observed, the principles and practices that sustain liberty are only realized in history when they become the 'habits of the heart' of a people.**

## Once More: Liberalism and Some Problems of Historical Transmission between the Generations

As the democratic age dawned, Tocqueville envisioned the possibility that democracies would drift away from freedom. As the democratic age may be coming to a close—I will leave to each of you to consider the symptoms of this demise—Tocqueville's concerns continue to haunt us. For what comes in the wake of democracy? Tocqueville thought it would be some form of despotism, and history seems to be realizing his prophetic fear.

We hoped that the advance of democracy over colonialism would bring advances in human freedom. Nevertheless, history has revealed to us story after story of promising democratic starts that soon gave way to illiberal dictatorships. In Africa and Latin America, especially, "democratic" processes continue to bring socialist-minded leaders to power. Why does this happen? Are young democracies fragile because they have bad ideas, bad institutions, or is it because new democratic citizens have not yet cultivated the deeply rooted and intergenerational habits of self-constraint that democratic governance requires?

And what of the so-called liberal democracies of Europe and the United States, which are no longer drifting but rushing headlong into softer despotisms? Why does a nation such as the United States, where liberty, equality, and prosperity blossomed, become a welfare-warfare state guided primarily by social democratic values?

Where do we go from here? If the experience of Europe is any guide, established liberal democracies are going to be followed by some form of global governance structures managed by "enlightened" technocrats and humanitarians who know better what is good for the rest of us.

Is such constitutional drift inevitable? Is the advance of liberty always to be just a short ride up one side of the Ferris wheel, followed as rapidly by the descent and a need once more, as Hayek says, to push the wheel back to the ascending motion? Does our liberal philosophy help us understand how we might escape such cycles of history? Perhaps we need "the historical way of thinking" to help guide us through the end of democracy and to discover a more steadily ascending path for human flourishing.

In a 1992 essay on "The Importance of Political Traditions," Leonard Liggio reminded us that historical study is essential to our understanding of contemporary political and cultural problems. He described how the nations of South America and North America developed so differently after 1492, even though both had inherited the legal and political institutions of medieval Europe. Quoting the legal historian Harold Berman, Liggio observed that even where democracies thrived in the Americas they largely abandoned "the law-creating role of the judiciary" and exalted the role of legislatures. Only the U.S. Constitution, with its deliberate recourse to medieval English institutions staved off democracy's drift for a while (1992: 13, 27–28).

Such study of comparative historical institutions is essential to the advance of liberty. But how much more might the historical way of thinking, rooted in humility and curiosity about our place in the flow of time, improve the ways we live out our liberal principles? Can the historical way of thinking deepen our theory of human action? Can it help us better sustain the liberal tradition?

## The Historical Way of Thinking

The English historian Herbert Butterfield was the teacher of my teacher John Pocock. Butterfield was also the author of *The Whig Interpretation of History* (1931), in which he called upon historians to try to understand human action in its own historical context and contingency. He argued that historians must avoid presentism: interpreting the past as if the actions of its actors aimed at us.

# Once More: Liberalism and Some Problems of Historical Transmission between the Generations

To approach our lives with historical awareness is to be open to exploring both the continuities and the discontinuities we have with the past. Through the historical way of thinking we come to better know ourselves; we learn to participate in keeping alive the traditions that are the core operating systems of our civilizations; and we prepare ourselves to recognize when either drift or revolutionary conditions necessitate creative and courageous action.

Good historical inquiry can also help us declare decisively that some ideas and institutions are more conducive to human betterment than others. Refusing to take a "Whiggish view" of history, as if we can see the causal steps in time's arrow, invites us to delve more deeply to understand the processes by which historical institutions and civilizations rise and fall.

In the Rede Lecture he delivered at Cambridge University in 1971, Butterfield speculated on "The *Discontinuities* between the Generations in History: Their Effect on the Transmission of Political Experience" (emphasis added). In this essay he imaginatively explored the question of how a people lose liberty.

> It seems that liberty is greatly prized by those who are struggling for it or who have recently lost it. But those who have inherited it come to depreciate it; for it can be a bother and an inconvenience. Some people are bored with anything of the sort; and at any rate the other man's freedom, everybody else's freedom, can be a nuisance to any of us.
>
> More important still, once you possess liberty you acquire the feeling that that particular problem is behind you, and you turn your real longings now to something else, something which is all the more valuable to you because you do not possess it. Having set your heart on this further object, you can convince yourself that liberty is mere luxury, and then it

becomes very easy to surrender to a Messiah who says he will give you the thing that you are now really wanting.

It becomes all the more easy in that you are siding with a winner—for the time being, you gain your object and the loss of liberty falls on the other party. In reality, this liberty that is being sacrificed is the freedom to choose your objective in the next stage in the story—it is the thing that brings men closest to a mastery over their own destiny (19).

Let's look at that last sentence again. For Butterfield, the freedom to choose our objective in the next stage in the story is the liberty that is meaningful.

## What of Hayek's Utopia?

It has occurred to me to ask: Does Butterfield shed light for us on Hayek's puzzle in his essay on "The Intellectuals and Socialism" as to why socialism gains momentum across the generations, and why he asserts that liberalism must be made to appeal *once more*?

Let's look at Hayek's statement in its larger context:

> We must make the building of a free society once more an intellectual adventure, a deed of courage. What we lack is a liberal Utopia, a program which seems neither a mere defense of things as they are nor a diluted kind of socialism, but a truly liberal radicalism which does not spare the susceptibilities of the mighty . . ., which is not too severely practical, and which does not confine itself to what appears today to be politically possible.

My intellectual journey with classical liberalism began with Hayek's "The Use of Knowledge in Society," so it is hard for me to admit that I have struggled with the use we have made of "The

Intellectuals and Socialism" in our community. My concerns are many, but, essentially, I think Hayek stumbled here over the fundamental challenge of reconciling liberalism as political philosophy and liberalism as a tradition of lived experience.

As readers of Hayek, we know that when men believe with a fatal conceit that they have the capacity to plan a Utopian renewal of the world, trouble often begins. The classical liberal certainly believes that working for social and policy reform to advance the freedom and prosperity of more people is necessary, but I think Hayek missteps when he suggests that what we need to win people to these reforms is "a liberal Utopia," a comprehensive program that can compete for public opinion with the socialist Utopias on offer everywhere.

Now, a Utopia is, of course, No Place. And aren't our hopes for liberalism that we can do more to make our lives better in This Place? What led Hayek to call for a Utopian vision for liberalism?

In "The Intellectuals and Socialism" Hayek proposed that socialist ideas appeal to a certain type of historical actor he calls intellectuals, the "professional secondhand dealers in ideas" whose influence over public opinion in the modern world has grown so strong that they have become "the governing force of politics." Hayek does not attribute evil motives to the intellectual class but observes how the visionary character of socialist Utopianism serves as a powerful pull to the young. And so, he proposes, liberalism needs some form of similar imaginative and compelling vision.

For over seventy years now, classical liberals have read Hayek's essay as a sort of recipe for how to advance "the philosophical foundations of a free society." We talk about the "structure of social change," as if we have a linear formula for converting ideas into policy, and we have built up an extensive network of organizations seeking to counter the entrenched influence of the intellectuals. Nevertheless, we have not seemed to loosen the allure of collectivist ideals.

So, what if Hayek's call for a liberal intellectual class bearing the standard for a "liberal Utopianism" misses the mark? What if liberalism must in fact be transmitted between the generations through a living tradition of political and entrepreneurial experience rather than pulled forward by an unrealizable Utopian vision? Wouldn't this possibility actually align better with Hayek's trenchant insights about spontaneous orders, the evolution of social institutions such as law and language, and the indispensable centrality of local knowledge in the processes of social cooperation?

**What if it is not a liberal Utopianism but a deeper understanding of the roles of culture and community in the processes of historical change that will better help us attract future generations away from socialism's redemptive promises of security, solidarity, and salvation?**

There seem to remain tensions in classical liberal thought between the need for liberal idealism and the necessity of liberal action grounded in that freedom we all should have to choose our own objective in the next stage in the story. What if it is not a liberal Utopianism but a deeper understanding of the roles of culture and community in the processes of historical change that will better help us attract future generations away from socialism's redemptive promises of security, solidarity, and salvation? Can we invite people step-by-step onto a path of different, more liberal-oriented, choices? I think so, but this is more likely to happen in community than in the trenches of political warfare.

## What Is the Role of the Practical Men?

In Hayek's essay there is another actor who appears briefly to whom we have not paid much attention. This is the "the practical man of affairs." Hayek is not very generous here to the practical men, suggesting that their "deep distrust of theoretical speculation" attracts them to what is "politically possible" instead of engaging them as supporters of the more "systematic policy for freedom" worked out by scholars.

Here we enter a debate enjoined by Liggio's longtime colleague Murray Rothbard. For decades, Rothbard called for a strategy of building up a libertarian "hard core" to advance the political goals of liberalism. Disdaining gradualism in theory, this hard core would hold out for only radical changes. Rothbard properly noted that "ideas do not spread and advance by themselves, in a social vacuum; they must be adopted and spread by people, people who must be convinced of and committed to the progress of liberty." He thus argued that "the advancement of liberty requires a movement as well as a body of ideas" (1977, 2).

Unfortunately, the strategy of advancing a "radical general system" through a Utopian liberal movement sits in philosophical and practical tension with the necessity people face to make a living and make a life in the world.

Is there a better way to understand the processes of historical change? A simple public choice analysis suggests that intellectuals gain influence in part because they capture the social institutions that provide them a living. From the platforms of the universities, the media, and the halls of legislative power they become the largest voice in public affairs. It is in their interest to shore up their influence in these institutions by excluding their critics.

Perhaps this, more than the Utopian appeal of socialism, accounts for the reason that since the early twentieth century liberal scholars have found it increasingly difficult to make a life or a living in the institutions that shape public opinion. This has meant that their continued work has depended on the building of new institutions, and thus, ironically, upon the philanthropy of practical men of affairs, the successful entrepreneurs who made their livings through the daily work of creating value by meeting the material and cultural demands of consumers.

In focusing too much on the limitations of the practical men and their tendencies to settle for gradual reforms in politics over radical revolutions, Hayek and Rothbard both seem to pass over the indispensable and strategic role of the entrepreneur in effecting the changes in society that people will either adopt or ignore in the marketplace.

Classical liberals scholars have, of course, deeply analyzed entrepreneurship, and we often celebrate the entrepreneurs among us. In this audience we often recount the remarkable story of Sir Antony Fisher's life, for example, admiring the young entrepreneur whose concerns with the advance of collectivism in Britain led him to discover the writings of Hayek, to learn new methods of chicken farming from Baldy Harper, and ultimately to found the institutions that would give birth to Atlas Network.

But we need to more deeply theorize the role of entrepreneurs in shaping the evolution of social institutions. Through their innovations and services to people, entrepreneurs shape the very landscape within which people choose their objectives in the next stage in the story. And so it matters very much what the entrepreneur believes about the nature of men and the nature of his power in the world, especially when he turns to philanthropic causes.

Why do some practical men—Antony Fisher, Pierre Goodrich, Manuel Ayau—readily see how collectivism constrains liberty and decide to devote their entrepreneurial energy and philanthropy to combat it? And why are so many more seduced by the humanitarian impulse that partners with malinvestment in constructivist social change?

Far from dismissing the practical men, liberalism needs to understand how to draw more of them in to delving beneath the shadows and mirrors of public opinion into deeper conversations about full scope of liberty and its benefits.

For over a decade, I had the pleasure of working alongside Dick Cornuelle in thinking through some of these challenges. Much as Leonard Liggio called our attention to the need for a deeper understanding of the Western legal tradition, Dick called for classical liberals to better understand humanity's very deep need for community, which underscores the prominent and problematic role of philanthropy in the Western tradition.

In 1991, after the fall of the Berlin Wall, Dick published an essay called "New Work for Invisible Hands" proposing that with the collapse of Soviet Communism, classical liberals would immediately need to confront the social democracy that had crept across the West by working "to understand voluntary social process as completely as we understand market process."

This meant we had to try to understand and advance the role of a philanthropic enterprise better informed by liberal principles, rooted in the belief that people must have freedom to choose their objectives in the next stage in the story and recognizing that community is something that emerges when "people come together to accomplish things that are important to them and succeed." Only through creative entrepreneurship to connect more people to the market order could we present "credible visions of alternatives to the failing programs of centrism" (1996, 10–11, 32–33).

In the decades since Cornuelle wrote those lines, we have made some progress along these lines. As Brad Lips catalogues in his new book, *Liberalism and the Free Society in 2021,* many of you are already in the business of finding entrepreneurial solutions for human betterment. But we still seem to be struggling to put the whole package together, to align our language and theory and practice into a distinctively liberal strategy that can stand against, and hopefully even turn, the prevailing winds of socialism that bear down upon us.

This brings us full circle to the problem of "once more." Why does it seem that liberalism is once more slipping behind instead of gaining momentum? In part, I think it is because, often in the name of philanthropy, our liberalism has become too entangled with the constructivist forms democracy took in the twentieth century, to the point that we, too, talk instrumentally about the theory and logic models of social change. But this is the very road to serfdom.

Hayek knew that to choose one's government did not ensure liberty. And as Vincent Ostrom reminded us: "Tocqueville's concern about Majority Despotism arises when those who exercise the prerogatives of Government attempt to cope with all the problems of life, sparing people the cares of thinking and the troubles of living" (26). Can we wrest back those responsibilities of community from today's Leviathans?

The hubris of "liberal democracy" spread a false and even Utopian humanitarianism across the world in the twentieth century.

Today we need a renewed vision of liberal constitutionalism. We have to embrace the hard work of spreading the ideas and institutions of limited government and rule of law, as we always have. And, more importantly in my opinion, we must offer a truly humane and historically perceptive vision that advocates the moral necessity of treating people as free to choose their own objectives in the next stage in the story.

As my colleague at UFM, Ramón Parellada, put it recently, in reflecting on the latest wave of government reactions to the pandemic:

## Once More: Liberalism and Some Problems of Historical Transmission between the Generations

People know how to take care of themselves. They are not stupid. They choose what suits them best according to their current situation, the moment of their life and the place where they are. To think that the government knows more than they do is fatal arrogance.

But we see such fatal arrogance all around us today. With social justice as the end, and "theories of social change" shaping the means, the NGO-industrial complex fueled by modern philanthropy—and its partnership with the liberal democratic administrative state—has largely deconstructed the constitutional arrangements and cultural restraints that define free societies. We need to look more critically upon this new hero called the "social entrepreneur" and his goal of promoting reform, often without counting the monetary or moral costs. That is the way not to Utopia but to Apocalypse.

In drawing my remarks to a close, I want to leave you with one big thought and a challenge.

The thought is this: The transmission of a liberal tradition must be a task of meaningful and iterative historical action toward human betterment rather than the pursuit of utopian dreams.

As Brad Lips puts it:

The future belongs to the advocates of authentic liberalism—open and entrepreneurial, inclusive and generous. We seek no end-state Utopia, but we know that it's through the iterative innovations of free people that societies will continue to enjoy improving standards of living and more opportunities to pursue happiness" (Lips, 178).

What are tradition and culture but the ideas, institutions, and habits of the heart that emerge from the iterative innovations and choices that people make in communities?

The advance of liberty needs a stable community of people, extending through the generations, who help one another discharge their responsibilities in light of the general principles of freedom.

So, we do have to teach the young these general principles and help them practice their application. I believe no educational institution is doing this better right now than UFM, which is why I am honored to be joining the executive team there. But even the teaching of general principles can take us only so far, because they don't always tell us exactly what to do.

In the complex social systems in which we live, we often face difficult choices with no one right answer. Each of us faces serious responsibilities and has to make a living in the world, fulfilling commitments to the diverse little platoons we make. Learning how to balance these responsibilities and to discharge them cannot be the work of ideas alone. It requires participation in a community bearing these principles in a robust tradition of lived experience and the wisdom of the "practical men" among us.

> **The transmission of a liberal tradition must be a task of meaningful and iterative historical action toward human betterment rather than the pursuit of utopian dreams.**

Classical liberals have long been the ardent champions of the creative powers of entrepreneurship. But more than ever we need to explain the difference between the unpredictable, kaleidic dynamism of a truly entrepreneurial world and the constructivist dreams of "social change." More than ever, we need the courage NOT to be Utopian.

We do need to cast a hopeful vision that can help the practical men, the entrepreneurs and policymakers among

## Once More: Liberalism and Some Problems of Historical Transmission between the Generations

us, act on the first anthropological and moral principle of liberalism: that humans can live with the freedoms and the responsibilities of choice, even in conditions of uncertainty and risk.

Because we are human beings, constrained by limited resources and given only a limited time to act in this world, Utopian movements have a certain appeal to us. But they do not serve us well.

Because we are human beings, constrained by limited resources and given only a limited time to act in this world, we need to understand the choices our ancestors faced and how their choices shaped the freedoms and the possibilities now open to us. And we need friends and mentors beside us in the flow of our lives to help us make the next best choices we can, hopefully in light of liberal principles.

On most days, the best any of us can do is to find the next logical step from where we are.

And herein is the challenge with which I want to leave you.

I told you at the beginning of my remarks about the important role Leonard Liggio played as a scholar and a mentor to so many of us. For Leonard, we were not replaceable cogs in a movement, but members of a community of persons bearing the image of God and having unique endowments.

Every good mentor I have ever had connected me to a tradition and then challenged me to extend and deepen it in order to accomplish the things I am uniquely here to understand and to do.

So I ask you now to think about your mentors. Who inspired you to join the adventure of living for liberty? Who has connected you to community, held you accountable when necessary, and helped you find the courage to move forward when the way looked cloudy?

And I challenge you to tell me: Who you are mentoring? With whom are you sharing the stories and lessons and ideas that shape your life's work? Are you helping a younger person take up their own role in the story?

This is how liberty will be transmitted through the generations. So be like Leonard, build these bridges!

**Bibliography**

Cornuelle, Richard C. (1965). *Reclaiming the American Dream: The Role of Private Individuals and Voluntary Associations*. New York: Random House.

_____ (1983). *Healing America*. New York: Putnam.

_____ (1991). "New work for invisible hands: A future for libertarian thought." The Times Literary Supplement. April 5, 1991.

_____ (1996). "De-nationalizing Community," Philanthropy

Cowen, Tyler (2003). "Entrepreneurship, Austrian Economics, and the Quarrel Between Philosophy and Poetry." The Review of Austrian Economics, 16:1, 5–23.

Ealy, Lenore T. (2013). "Can Civil Society Save Us?" The Freeman. August 28, 2013. Accessed March 20, 2019 at https://fee.org/articles/can-civil-society-save-us/.

_____ (2014). "The Intellectual Crisis in Philanthropy," Society, Vol 51, No 1 (Jan/Feb 2014), 87-96. doi:10.1007/s12115-013-9741-2.

_____ (2011). "Richard C. Cornuelle and the Revolution of Social Responsibility," Society, Vol 48, No 6, 510-516.

Ealy, Lenore T. and Steven D. Ealy (2006). "Progressivism and Philanthropy." The Good Society (15): 35-42.

Hayek, F. A. (1949). "The Intellectuals and Socialism." The University of Chicago Law Review. Spring 1949: 417-20, 421-23, 425-433. Reprinted in George B. de Huszar, ed., *The Intellectuals: A Controversial Portrait*. Glencoe, Illinois: The Free Press, 1960.

Liggio, Leonard (1992). "The Importance of Political Traditions." Johannesburg: Free Market Foundation. pp 12-32.

Lips, Brad (2021). *Liberalism and the Free Society in 2021*. Arlington, Virginia: Atlas Economic Research Foundation.

Ostrom, Vincent (1997) *The Meaning of Democracy and the Vulnerability of Democracies: A Response to Tocqueville's Challenge*. Ann Arbor: University of Michigan.

Rothbard, Murray N. (1977). *Toward a Strategy for Libertarian Social Change. Private Memorandum.* Accessed at December 2, 2021, at: http://davidmhart.com/liberty/AmericanLibertarians/Rothbard/Strategy/1977TowardStrategyLibertarianSocialChange.html

_____(1994). "A New Strategy for Liberty." Rothbard-Rockwell Report (October 1994). Accessed December 2, 2021, at: http://davidmhart.com/liberty/AmericanLibertarians/Rothbard/Strategy/1994NewStrategy.html

Shackle, G.L.S. (1979). *Imagination and the Nature of Choice*. Edinburgh: Edinburgh University Press.

Vaughn, Karen I. (2018 [1994]). "Can democratic society reform itself? The limits of constructive change." In Boettke, Peter J. and David L. Prychitko, The Market Process. Arlington, Virginia: Mercatus Center, pp. 229-243.

9

# PRESERVING LIBERALISM AMID EMERGENCIES

By Gabriel Calzada Álvarez

---

The tenth Liggio Lecture was given on November 16, 2022, in New York City, by Gabriel Calzada Álvarez. Gabriel used his lecture to encourage the classical liberal community to recognize the losses to freedom that occur during emergencies, such as the COVID-19 pandemic that we lived through in recent years. He draws lessons from history that might inform strategies for retaining individual liberties in the face of future crises.

Gabriel first came to Atlas Network as the executive director of Spain's Instituto Juan de Mariana. He served as the Rector of Universidad Francisco Marroquín in Guatemala from 2015 to 2021, before returning to his native Canary Islands to launch the Universidad de las Hespérides in 2022. He was elected president of Mont Pelerin Society one month before giving this Liggio Lecture.

---

We have been living through a chain of crises and emergencies since the beginning of the twenty-first century. Just when we seem to be emerging from one crisis, a new emergency presents itself unexpectedly. The diagnoses of crises, and the measures taken in response, will shape our interpretation of this historical experience, as well as the course of history itself. Crises are not always stochastically independent events; oftentimes, despite differing in nature, they share common factors. In this first quarter of the twenty-first century, we have suffered the dot com crisis, the terrorist crisis, the mortgage and credit crunch crisis of the Great Recession, the climate crisis, the COVID-19 pandemic, the Second Gulf War, the war in Ukraine, the economic crisis of 2022, and the current energy crisis—to mention only the most striking. The outburst of successive crises has triggered official and unofficial declarations of emergency, each initiating a new debate on the limits of individual freedom. The kind of society that we will live in for the next hundred or more years depends on the narrative that results from those debates.

The relationship between freedom and crises is a tense one, with each new crisis calling into question some aspect of individual freedom for supposedly limiting effective counteractive action. Moreover, at least in the last century, crises have fueled the growth of the state—both in its size and sphere of action—diminishing the sphere of the exercise of personal liberties. To add to the complexity, this process is often set in motion by politicians who claim to act in *defense* of fundamental rights and freedoms.[1]

Is it possible to avoid the degradation of individual liberties and the growth of statism with each new emergency? Is it possible to preserve liberalism amidst successive crises and emergencies of diverse kinds? These are crucial, high-stakes questions for classical liberals to address.

**The Breeding Ground**

Emergencies and crises create an ideal breeding ground for the growth of the state and for the dissolution of individual freedom. When a crisis is perceived, the role of the state shines and its legitimacy grows, thanks to the public's fears, its desire for protection, and the urgent need to join forces and pool resources to face an existential threat. Objections to the state's interventions in people's private lives come to be received as a kind of blasphemy that threatens our peaceful coexistence.

---

[1] See Robert Higgs (1987). *Crisis and Leviathan: Critical Episodes in the Growth of the State.* Pacific Research Institute.

It does not seem unreasonable to hypothesize that the origin of the state may be related to crises and emergencies.[2] According to this hypothesis, the state's coercive form of social organization would have outcompeted other forms of social organization in critical scenarios such as wars, pandemics, and other emergencies, allowing for the survival of the groups and societies that sustained it. At the same time, those groups and societies that were coordinated around other institutional arrangements—ones that might be more effective for various other purposes but less effective in warfare—were absorbed or eliminated. Perhaps that is why the Spanish philosopher José Ortega y Gasset stated that "[t]he State is, above all, a producer of security (the security from which the mass-man is born, let us not forget). That is why it is, above all, an army."[3]

The state today is almost universally the form by which public affairs are administrated, especially the provision of defense and security services in the face of emergencies. The above hypothesis could account for why. At the same time, it could explain from the supply side why the state grows most notably when the prevailing conditions are those of conflicts, crises, and emergencies.[4]

The government's demand also seems to grow in times of conflict and crisis. "Imagine," says Ortega y Gasset, "that any difficulty, conflict or problem arises in the public life of a country: the mass-man will tend to demand that the State immediately assume it, that it be directly in charge of resolving it with its gigantic and incontrovertible means. ... When the masses feel some misfortune ... it is a great temptation for them that permanent and

---

[2] See Bruce D. Porter (1994), War and the Rise of the State. *The Military Foundations of Modern Politics*; Martin L. Van Creveld (1999), *The Rise and Decline of the State*; and Charles Tilly (1985), "War Making and State Making as Organized Crime."

[3] José Ortega y Gasset (1926), *La Rebelión de las Masas*.

[4] See Higgs (1987) and Porter (1994).

sure possibility of achieving everything—without effort, struggle, doubt, or risk—without more than touching the spring and making the portentous machine work."[5]

Perhaps the collective memory of the state's origin leads many people to respond to moments of extreme uncertainty by embracing collective action through its coercive apparatus. Perhaps it is simply the easy and obvious answer for those searching for an agent that is capable of removing the responsibility of life and death decisions from the citizen. It could be that it is the most obvious way to provide a unified response without the bickering that typically comes with collective decisions under stress. Perhaps there is no other arrangement or social apparatus that gathers so much power behind which to feel protected and avoid having to directly bear the responsibility of making decisions or of assuming opportunity cost.

In any case, since its origin, the state has been expanding its niche in society in response to natural disasters and political, social, and economic crises. These situations are fertile ground for an expansive state, with its competitive advantage based on the use of organized violence. An institution whose natural sphere of action is the provision of security, whether it be through defense or attack, can enforce conformity, so people fall in line with one plan forward.

However, what we truly need in an emergency is not conformity. We need logistical expertise. We need technological innovation. We need subtle and creative thinking. If we compare the fruits of voluntary cooperation networks in these areas with those of the state, the state's competitive advantage vanishes. This fact, however, has not stopped the state from penetrating deep into the provision of multiple services where it performs poorly. Through prices well

---

5  Ortega y Gasset (1926), p. 110.

below the marginal cost of production or through the threat of coercion, the state has been able to enter sectors where technology, logistics, and creativity are fundamental, such as education and healthcare.

The sphere of coercion and the sphere of voluntariness are antagonistic. The more hegemonic ties, the less contractual ties; the more coercive relationships, the less voluntary relationships; the more impositions, the less freedom; more state, less market. Public education (both through provision and through regulation) reduces the space for private initiative; government provision of "free" healthcare, sustained by taxes, hinders the private provision of it; the public organization of security and defense reduces the possibilities of contractual provision of these services. It is not the subject of this essay to analyze how many and what kind of limits the state must have so that the free market can exist and develop, if it needs it to some extent and in some way; how much coercion is necessary for voluntary relationships to flourish; how many hegemonic ties are needed for contractual ties to constitute the main network of relationships in a society.[6]

> **What we truly need in an emergency is not conformity. We need logistical expertise. We need technological innovation. We need subtle and creative thinking. If we compare the fruits of voluntary cooperation networks in these areas with those of the state, the state's competitive advantage vanishes.**

---

[6] On this question, see Murray N. Rothbard (1970), *Power and Market*; and Robert Nozick (1974), *Anarchy, State, and Utopia*.

I want to focus this Liggio Lecture on how to avoid the decline of freedoms in the face of these dynamics. What can we do to protect personal freedoms in times of peril? How can we introduce cooperation, voluntariness, and contractual solutions in areas that might be vulnerable to state intervention during a crisis?[7]

## The Problem of the Statist Approach to Crisis and Emergencies

The dangers that threaten freedom in times of crisis are diverse. They include the concentration of executive power in a few hands, resulting in decisions uninformed by contrary views; arbitrariness in the use of power, thereby weakening of the rule of law; temporary suspension of individual freedoms; perpetuation of "temporary" interventionist measures; tyranny of the experts; and the changing of rules to favor the work of those who manage the state apparatus.

In times of crisis, conflict, emergency, and whenever a sense of existential threat prevails, the population demands not just governmental solutions but a "strong government" with special powers for singularly complicated times. That strength is typically achieved through the concentration of resources, the centralization of political power, and greater laxity in the collective decision-making process by the executive branch. One way or another, the growth of political power is served on a plate that we surely know will not be to everyone's tastes.

---

7   This dynamic is explored in Ludwig von Mises (2001), *Crítica del Intervencionsimo. El Mito de la Tercera Vía*. Also, Ortega y Gasset (1926), p. 111, describes the consequences of this dynamic: "The result of this trend will be fatal. Social spontaneity will be violated time and time again by the intervention of the State; no new seed will be able to bear fruit. Society will have to live for the State; man, for the government machine. And since in the end it is nothing more than a machine whose existence and maintenance depend on the surrounding vitality that maintains it, the State, after sucking the marrow out of society, will remain skeletal, dead with that rusty death of the machine, much more cadaverous than that of the living organism."

The almost exclusive focus on a priority objective generates a tendency towards centralization. Decentralization is associated with the dispersed use of resources, while centralization is associated with the concentration of resources in one line of action. In turn, this greater concentration of resources in the hands of a small group who have not produced them, and who do not personally derive any economic or legal benefit from their proper use, is the perfect recipe for irresponsible use of the resources, in every possible sense of the adjective.

The centralization of decision-making means that personal freedoms are weakened, at least during the duration of the emergency. Often the curtailment of freedoms for an exceptional moment becomes a continuous questioning of the desirability of their very existence. This is how "emergency powers intended to save a constitution may grow into concentrated powers directed towards the destruction of the constitution."[8]

Urgency makes time seem scarcer than ever. To save time, the government is allowed to rule without following the processes created for the prevention of abuses in the use of power. This concession of greater latitude in the use of coercion is exercised by the person or body in which the concentration of resources has materialized. We are faced with a helmsman, a guide, a leader, a caudillo, a dictator who will implement the solution in a centralized manner, directing a large number of resources in accordance with a single action plan, the purpose of which is the dissipation of the danger that fuels the emergency. This way of governing is so comfortable for those who execute the political action that they not only have no incentive to put an end to the situation that allows it, but they have even a positive incentive to extend it.

---

[8] Carl J. Friedrich. (1968), "Constitutional Dictatorship and Emergency Powers" in *Constitutional Government and Democracy*, p. 570.

## Preserving Liberalism amid Emergencies

The demand for immediacy in decision-making makes it appropriate to govern through decrees and exceptional executive measures. By their very nature, these actions face fewer formal requirements that normally would ensure the just use of state powers. In the words of Benjamin Constant, "Once its methods have been admitted at all, they are found so quick, so convenient, that it seems no longer worthwhile to use any other. Presented initially as a last resort to be used only in infinitely rare circumstances, arbitrariness becomes the solution for all problems and an everyday expedient."[9] Once the government becomes accustomed to solving problems with that liberality in command, it becomes tedious to use other, more warranted procedures.

Because governments have greater discretion after declarations of emergencies, and they have less incentive to safeguard individual liberties, we must ask which is more dangerous: the cure or the disease? Carl Friedrich lends attention to this important question when he states that "it will always be a matter of judgment, a matter of weighing risks as to which is more dangerous: the threatening emergency or the powers for combating it."[10] An important question at this point is that of whose judgment is relevant to this question. Will it be the same group of people who will exercise the emergency powers? As we will see below, different societies have given different answers over time to this question.

---

9  Benjamin Constant (1988), *Political Writings*. Edited by and translated by Biancamaria Fontana, p. 292.

10  Carl J. Friedrich (1968), p. 581.

In some situations, the concentration of power and discretion is such that government leaders will believe their desired ends justify almost any means, now legitimized (or at least legalized) during an emergency. They believe they have carte blanche for measures such as confiscation, special taxes, unlimited public indebtedness, and extraordinary inflation. The harmful effects of these policies on the public welfare and on the enjoyment of fundamental freedoms are far-reaching and long-lasting, often much longer than the emergency itself.

Because the sacrifices of the population are very high—and to reinforce the idea that the end justifies the means and the probability of success justifies the imposed costs—it becomes necessary to remove any shadow of doubt about the appropriateness of the government's strategy and the policies it has dictated. To this end, what could be better than the creation of a committee of "wise" men, a group of experts who are in possession of the winning formula, who confirm that the chosen roadmap is the winning one and who therefore constrain the citizenry to follow orders for their own good. Each member of the expert committee knows the winning formula. There is no such thing as dissent—at least in the public eye. The expert committee concludes each meeting with an unequivocal recommendation.

Unfortunately, the possibility of error is high when betting everything on a single card. It is even higher if the incentives are not well aligned. And error in the case of emergencies manifests itself in losses of property, losses of days of freedom, and sometimes in losses of human lives.

In moments of emergency, the preciousness of time often makes more time-consuming decision-making processes less favored than quick ones. Solutions reached through a competitive process of trial and error seem impractical and inefficient compared to solutions reached by the decision of a small group of people who are presumed to have a great deal of knowledge concerning the problem, its diagnosis, and its solution. Their collective wisdom should not be questioned or doubted, even by each other. This is why meetings of expert committees take place behind closed doors, and their conclusions are presented without an accounting of trade-offs, with only one optimal way forward. The free market is no longer a reasonable vehicle for finding solutions. Trial and error by voluntary means is invalidated and unnecessary because of the expert committee that subscribes to a single recipe.

The state's measures also alter the market prices that are the guide to economizing resources in pursuit of overcoming the emergency. Especially in cases in which a "temporary" crisis becomes prolonged—and officials have every incentive to prolong it—the distortion of prices will be an added consequence of the state's solution to the emergency. Without the free prices typical of voluntary exchanges within a framework of respect for private property, there is no possibility of carrying out the economic calculation that shows which lines of use of resources generate value and which lines destroy it.[11]

Emergencies and crises often require a sudden change in the productive structure. Resources that were previously used to make shirts must now be used to make masks. Engines that were previously used to move windshields will now be used for assisted venti-

> **Especially in cases in which a "temporary" crisis becomes prolonged—and officials have every incentive to prolong it—the distortion of prices will be an added consequence of the state's solution to the emergency.**

11  See Ludwig von Mises (1920), *Die Wirtschaftsrechnung im sozialistischen Gemeinwesen*, and Jesús Huerta de Soto (2010), *Socialism, Economic Calculation, and Entrepreneurship*.

lation systems. Ignorance of spontaneous social orders encourages a belief that structures that evolved to serve a particular role can be easily redesigned for new circumstances. This constructivist vision of society leads to dirigisme and paternalism as it sees in the free market and globalization the causes of a society that they judge to be adrift.

Many emergency measures arrive with the adjective of "temporary," but then they refuse to disappear, even once the emergency is over. Agencies and departments created under extraordinary circumstances tend to justify their permanence and become an ongoing part of the state apparatus. As we have seen above, the exceptionality itself and the temporary curtailment of freedoms tend to be perpetuated. Once enough people live off the new powers and the new state budget, commissions become departments, decrees become laws, and temporary measures become permanent solutions. Even when the emergency is defused, the size and scope of the state do not return to their pre-crisis levels. The retreat of state expansion is more modest than its growth during the fight against the crisis. This has come to be called the ratchet effect, documented in detail by Robert Higgs in his pathbreaking *Crisis and Leviathan*. It seems this was the story of the last century.[12]

Higgs's grim conclusion seems to be that of someone who has discovered a curse impossible to dispel: "We know that other great crises will come. Whether they will be occasioned by foreign wars, economic collapse, or rampant terrorism, no one can predict with assurance. Yet in one form or another, great crises will surely come again, as they have from time to time throughout

---

12  Richard Posner disagrees with Robert Higgs when he argues, in relation to the war on terror, that "when the emergencies ended, civil liberties were restored, and later they were enlarged. There was no ratchet; the only ratchet under consideration derives from the contention by civil libertarians that an expansion of liberties must never be reversed." Richard A. Posner (2003). *Law, Pragmatism, and Democracy*, p. 304.

all human history. When they do, governments almost certainly will gain new powers over economic and social affairs. Everything that I have argued and documented in the preceding chapters points towards this conclusion. For those who cherish individual liberty and a free society, the prospect is deeply disheartening."[13]

The characteristics of emergencies are such that they require immediate resources, invite centralization of decisions, and promote the tyranny of experts. Statism and interventionism grow amid crises because the demands for immediacy and the centralization of power encourage the use of violence, the increased control of people, the limitation of freedoms, the abuse of power, and conversion of the temporary into the permanent. Under these conditions, the state apparatus grows with each new crisis and rarely returns to its previous course when the emergency is over.

Is there anything that can be done? Can we learn from the past? Or are we doomed to live in a more statist society for as long as we continue to witness times of crisis?

## The State's Competitive Advantages or Why the Statist Solution Persists

In order to respond to this dynamic of loss of freedoms in times of crisis, we must first understand why, time and time again, crises empower the state and those who govern it, despite the numerous observable problems and despite all the dangers entailed in the statist approach to emergency situations. What are the characteristics of handling emergencies that the state seems to be able to provide better than other forms of social organization? What are the characteristics of the state that have made it competitive? What is the issue to be solved and for which the state seems to have an irresistible offer?

---

[13] Higgs (1987), p. 262

The state apparatus, the monopoly on the use of violence, is capable of marshalling a large number of resources, to do so with immediacy, and to direct them to a specific purpose. These characteristics make the state a particularly competitive form of public organization when it comes to providing defense against existential dangers.

Emergencies usually require a large number of resources—and a large number of resources *now*—to be amassed and applied to dissipate the danger in question. The material resources to fight the emergency will have to come out of the means available through the restriction of consumption, the intensification of production, and the consumption of previously accumulated capital.[14] If today you do not manage to sacrifice resources that were originally being saved for tomorrow, perhaps tomorrow will not come. If we do not sacrifice consumption for other purposes in order to contribute resources to dissipate the emergency, perhaps there may no longer be any future consumption to satisfy. The form of social organization that manages to quickly and efficiently gather a large number of present resources and dedicate them to an objective (e.g., to combat an existential danger) will have a better chance of surviving over time. The apparatus that exercises the monopoly of legal coercive action that we know as the state has an enormous capacity to achieve this rapid gathering of a large number of resources through the threat of violence against those who do not wish to cooperate with the government's action plan.

---

14  There is a resemblance here to Mises's idea, expounded in Mises [1919] 1983, p. 166 and Mises 1918, p. 8. according to which "[w]ar can be waged only with weapons that are already on hand; One can take everything needed for war only from wealth already on hand. From the economic point of view, the present generation wages war, and it must also bear all material costs of war. Future generations are also affected only insofar as they are our heirs and we leave less to them than we would have been able to leave without the war's intervening. Whether the state now finances the war by debts or otherwise can change nothing about this fact. That the greatest part of the war costs was financed by state loans in no way signifies a shifting of war burdens onto the future but only a particular principle of distributing the war costs."

As we saw in the previous section, the importance often given to decentralization in times of sustained growth disappears when there is a generalized perception of crisis or emergency. The perceived positive effects of competition come to be seen as a luxury for times of certainty and prosperity, whereas centralization of resources is "needed" for the sake of emergency decision-making.

Once the resources have been gathered, the emergency requires their use against the danger. There is little point in amassing resources if they are not going to be deployed to end the emergency. The situation requires a complete focus on a specific course of action, very different from what happens in a free market in which owners of resources continually weigh the merits of different avenues for making progress.

Just as an organism may repel a disease by turning off parts of its functions to focus resources on life-saving tasks, the state apparatus can prohibit certain sectors' activities that it deems counter-productive to the fight against the crisis or emergency. This centralizing and planning dynamic invites the creation or reinforcement of a single executive command, which can extinguish possible internal divisions and bring order to the chaos that emerges; market prices are altered as a result of government intervention.[15]

Urgency requires speed in decision-making. A declaration of exceptional circumstances provides the means to accelerate and simplify public decision-making processes, so nothing interferes with the execution of the plan with which the collected resources will be used. Surely that is why "every modern constitution has recognized the problem of temporary emergencies and has sought to provide for a temporary concentration of powers to be used

---

15  Ludwig von Mises (1922), *Die Gemeinwirtschaft: Untersuchungen über den Sozialismus*.

in overcoming such emergencies."[16] Without the declaration of exceptionality, it is difficult to imagine how a society might organize its resources to fight against the clock trying to halt the threats caused by crises and emergencies.

The fear of a substantially worse future state of affairs, the urgent need for a solution, the desire to adapt the visible structure of production, the tendency to centralize decision-making power, and the deference to perceived experts are a set of forces that lead to the strengthening of the state apparatus in times of great uncertainty, emergency, and crisis. Because of the state's monopoly on the use of violence—and its ability to quickly gather large amounts of resources and direct them to a specific purpose—it has an advantage in responding to the public demand for defense against existential dangers.

### *A classical liberal approach to crisis and emergencies*

So how should we envision a liberal push-back against the growth of statism in times of crisis? We must do more than simply call attention to the risks of authoritarianism, even totalitarianism, that materialize with state intervention. We must demonstrate that the voluntary institutional arrangements can provide superior safeguards against emergent crises. To do this, we might begin where I imagine Leonard would advise: tracing alternatives that have worked throughout history, to solve through cooperation and contracts the problems that statism addresses imperfectly through centralization and violence.

As happens in general with institutional arrangements, statist solutions will only cease to exist when they are overcome. Prohibition of government interventions in emergencies will not work without a new arrangement that fulfills the function for which the

---

16   Carl J. Friedrich (1968), p. 558.

state body was created. It is necessary to overcome, not naively eliminate, the chain of statist responses to emergencies that shrink the sphere of individual freedom. If alternatives are not implemented, we may be faced with a growing scope of action and interference by the state to the detriment of individual liberties and the free market.

## Learning from History

When societies fail to prepare for emergency circumstances, they risk falling into arbitrariness and chaos. If there is a lack of institutional arrangements for containing the accumulation of power during emergencies, statism may advance. This fact is so well understood that using emergencies as a Trojan horse has been one of the preferred entry routes for authoritarian political movements, such as communism or fascism. "[These] have created in the past and continue to create a state of universal emergency throughout the world community by their appeal to force. As the *Communist Manifesto* made clear, and as the masters of the Soviet Union and Communist China have repeatedly reaffirmed, their appeal is to revolutionary force. We have seen at the outset of this chapter that war and insurrection create the states of emergency which call for the establishment of constitutional dictatorship."[17]

Aware of how lack of preparedness for emergencies could erode freedoms and open the way to tyranny, classical liberal authors such as Juan de Mariana advised that societies should prepare in peacetime for possible dangers, and during crises and war, efforts should focus on returning to normality, stability, and peace.

Mechanisms must be established to clearly limit the use of concentrated powers. In the words of Carl Friedrich:

---

17  Carl J. Friedrich (1968), p. 580.

To overcome the emergency and to maintain constitutional government intact ... there must be a broad grant of powers, subject to equally strong limitations as to who shall exercise such powers, when, for how long, and to what extent.[18]

We may take inspiration from the example of the Roman dictatorship, "a political phenomenon whereby, in time of crisis, an eminent citizen was called upon by the ordinary officials of a constitutional republic, and was temporarily granted absolute power over its whole life, not to subvert but to defend the republic, its constitution, and its independence."[19]

This institutional arrangement was instituted shortly after the establishment of the Roman Republic and disappeared with it. In a way, it reintroduced the then recently abolished figure of a monarchical government for the exclusive case of governing during emergencies, when the counterweights of the republican system might prevent timely decision-making. During the three hundred years that it lasted, the institution of the Roman dictator was used ninety times, mainly for military emergencies, but also for biological ones, such as plagues. On no occasion was absolute power used to subvert the constitutional order.

> **Classical liberal authors such as Juan de Mariana advised that societies should prepare in peacetime for possible dangers, and during crises and war, efforts should focus on returning to normality, stability, and peace.**

---

18   Carl J. Friedrich (1968), p. 565.

19   Clinton L. Rossiter (1948), *Constitutional Dictatorship—Crisis Government in the Modern Democracies.* p. 16

To understand the success of the institution, it is convenient to analyze its four main characteristics: the appointment of a dictator was carried out according to precise constitutional processes; the dictatorship was instituted by persons other than the dictator himself; the duration of the exceptional situation had precise and strict limits; the objective of establishing the dictatorship was always to defend the constitutional order.

Some similarities between the Roman institution designed for moments of emergency and the modern constitutional resources of exceptionality are immediately apparent. "Like the Roman Republican dictatorship, martial rule, emergency powers, and the state of siege are all conceived in terms of maintaining a constitutional system rather than destroying it (until they are perverted into a usurpation of concentrated powers)."[20]

However, the second and third characteristics (that the emergency cannot be declared by whomever is going to govern it and that the times are precise and strictly limited) are rarely incorporated in modern legislation dealing with emergencies. And yet, they are two enormously effective characteristics when it comes to avoiding unnecessary claims to exceptional powers (by removing the temptation to declare a state of emergency to acquire special powers) and avoiding the persistence of the measures and bodies established to combat the emergency.

Let us imagine that, at the moment of declaring a state of emergency, rulers had to relinquish the exercise of power for the entire duration of the emergency, ceding the government and special powers to someone they neither chose nor control. Would the emergency that arose with the terrorist attacks of September 11, 2001, have given way to the wars launched under its shadow? I hypothesize the response might have been more contained and

---

20  Carl J. Friedrich (1968), p. 560.

wiser. Instead we live in a reality in which, two months ago, President Joe Biden renewed the status of the national emergency President George W. Bush first declared twenty-one years ago. Similarly, we have multitudes of democratic countries still in official states of emergency three years after the outbreak of the COVID-19 pandemic. I doubt this would be the case if the incentives to declare and extend an emergency in the first quarter of this century had been less potent.

Simple measures, such as limitations on who can exercise exceptional powers and for what durations, could alter the incentive system that has put at risk individual freedoms and constitutional orders. Instead, such powers tend to be renewed, and emergency measures are maintained over time, applied homogeneously without apparent cost-benefit analysis. With each new step, the politician who has assumed emergency powers believes he has saved the country from disaster. He finds justification to maintain the measures, commissions, and departments, regardless of their true effectiveness, and to renew the emergency status that allows him to "save the country" over and over again. Benjamin Constant observed this dynamic with his usual wit: "Certainly, we should have been adequately convinced by this, that a country saved every day in this manner must be a country that will soon be ruined."[21]

> **Simple measures, such as limitations on who can exercise exceptional powers and for what durations, could alter the incentive system that has put at risk individual freedoms and constitutional orders.**

---

21  Benjamin Constant (1988), p. 138.

## Savings, entrepreneurship, bonds, and insurance

Those who value freedom must demonstrate voluntary methods of gathering the vast amounts of resources usually required to face the dangers that emergencies bring—whether its source is an invading army, a virus, a meteorite, or a relatively sudden change of temperatures. In addition, if the emergency or crisis cannot be dissipated with the initially available resources, it will be essential to have an economic system that allows for the production of necessary materials. Fundamentally, it is necessary to have a culture of savings. Postponing consumption in order to have additional resources for an emergency is one of the simplest, most obvious, and most immediate ways of preparing for threats to social harmony, and more generally, for risk and uncertainty.

By refraining from consuming some of our resources in the present, we find ourselves with more resources in the future than we otherwise would have; that is, more resources than we would have if we had consumed them. In this way, those who save are in a better position to face harmful effects from events whose occurrence is subject to chance. Savings—understood as an investment in the most liquid assets on the market—constitutes safe resources available at the desired time to deal with possible unforeseen events and emergencies. It is important to recognize that, while postponing consumption naturally increases resources for possible future emergencies, the degree of liquidity of those resources will largely determine the extent to which they can actually be used to lessen the uncertainty and threat.[22]

---

22  The liquidity of an asset (i.e., the extent to which its disposal can be achieved without suffering losses of value or time) depends on several characteristics, as described by Carl Menger, in his seminal 1892 article, "On the origin of money," translated by Caroline A. Foley, *The Economic Journal*, 2(6), p. 239–255. Characteristics include: 1) the number of persons in want of the commodity in question, 2) the purchasing power of those persons, 3) the availability of the commodity in relation to the unsupplied want; 4) the divisibility of the asset; 5) the politically and socially imposed limitations on exchange or consumption of the commodity. The article goes on to also expose the spatial and temporal limits of the salability of assets.

Here it is important to note that government action in times of emergency is not financed with resources it has saved; what it regularly extracts from the citizenry is immediately spent. This lack of savings at the state level stems from the belief that saving is a useless and even harmful activity. According to this way of seeing things, demand is what drives economic progress, whereas savings reduce the potential level of demand. Why save when you can always demand extraordinary resources from the taxpayer? Based on this premise, it is not surprising that the state discourages frugality with a seemingly endless number of charges and penalties, from taxation to inflation. Of course, a culture of savings is something that civil society needs to develop, and should be able to without great difficulty if the electorate clearly reveals that preference. The preservation of freedoms in times of crisis may depends on creating and sustaining a more responsible orientation toward savings and investment.

In a society with a strong savings culture, the issuance of bonds is an ideal instrument through which large amounts of resources can be pooled and directed on a voluntary basis. This way of channeling resources has the advantage that citizens can decide which dangers, crises, and emergencies they consider serious enough to require that the resources be saved.

The issuance of emergency bonds to the public has the virtue of being a non-redistributionist approach to financing a fight against a perceived emergency. It allows the free market to work as well as possible under the extreme conditions of a crisis. Bonds—even in the form of state bonds, i.e., state borrowing from the public—were economist Ludwig von Mises's preferred way of financing emergencies and war as, in his eyes, war bonds are not endowed with the unlucky consequences of the alternative financing tools.[23]

Reflecting on the First World War, Mises wrote that the state covered the largest part of the war costs by incurring state debt and contracting state loans. He first rejected the common assumption that this resulted in a redistribution that favors capitalists, claiming that it makes possible for the owners of industries and landowners to afford their part of the cost, without having to sell their capital goods during tough times to the capitalists who are in a liquid position at the moment. He then showed that, if these owners of non-movable capital had to access private credit to pay for the war taxes, "land and homeowners would have had to pay more interest on their private debts than they had to pay indirectly in interest on the State debt."[24]

In his defense of state loans through war bonds as the best way to finance a war, Mises also rejected the "generation argument," which professes that this way of financing a war shifts the costs of war from the present generation onto future ones. In doing this, he revises his famous claim that "[w]ar can be waged only with present goods," and proceeds to argue that "[one] can fight only with weapons that are already on hand; one can take everything needed for war only from wealth already on hand. From the economic point of view, the present generation wages war, and

---

23  Murray Rothbard had a very different position when it came to the financing of war or any other emergency through state bonds. For him the purchase of state bonds is always "a voluntary participation in future confiscation to be committed by the government" Rothbard (1993), p. 882. Rothbard also asserted that "there is nothing very patriotic about buying a bond, with the assurance that the principal will be returned, and that you will obtain a safe interest income out of the already burdened taxpayers. Moreover, these funds would mainly come out of savings, funds which otherwise would have been invested in industry" Rothbard (1950), p. 3.

24  Mises (1983), p. 167.

it must also bear all material costs of war. Future generations are also affected only insofar as they are our heirs and we leave less to them than we would have been able to leave without the war's intervening. Whether the state now finances the war by debts or otherwise can change nothing about this fact. That the greatest part of the war costs was financed by state loans in no way signifies a shifting of war burdens onto the future but only a particular principle of distributing the war costs."[25] Private emergency bonds would have all the advantages that Mises proposes, while being a completely voluntary system.

As we explore other ways to avoid state intervention during emergencies, we can celebrate the capacities of private sector entities to play roles sometimes claimed by the state. Anti-terrorist actions could be realized by private defense agencies in the same way that they are used to protect important politicians in conflict zones. Large-scale humanitarian relief, whether responding to natural disasters or socio-political tensions, could be carried out by Blackwater-style security agencies rather than governments' armies. In fact, as Leonard Liggio explained in his illuminating article "American Foreign Policy and National-Security Management," the military's meddling in these types of civil issues helps explain the evolution and growth of interventionism on a global scale.[26] Opening this market (i.e., decriminalizing cross-border for-profit activities to ameliorate the suffering from crises) would attract capital and spur innovation in a sector dominated by the state's militarist formula. Rather than using brute force to restrict citizens from acting freely to combat the virus, terrorism, and economic dislocations, private actors might find new ways to align incentives for more positive results.

---

25 Mises (1983), p. 166. See also Mises (1918), p. 8.

26 Leonard P. Liggio (1972), "American Foreign Policy and National-Security Management," in *A New History of Leviathan; Essays on the Rise of the American Corporate State*.

This would mark a return to historical norms. For centuries, protection against major emergencies was carried out by civil society without significant participation by the state. As was the case with the privateers of the North American revolution or the soldiers that defended the free towns of the Hanseatic League, the defense against all kinds of aggressors has been led in the past by voluntary associations.

The support of private institutions has also been critical in the resolution of pandemics. The Metropolitan Life Insurance Company funded the American Public Health Association's Committee on the Statistical Study of the Influenza Epidemic and "gave grants to university scientists and actually subsidized both the city of New York and the federal government, giving grants for research by Park and Williams in their New York laboratories and by George McCoy of the Public Health Service's Hygienic Laboratory."[27]

The Rockefeller Institute sponsored for decades the work of Avery, Dochez, Thomas Rivers, Florey, and Chain, among others, whose works would result in break-through discoveries in relation to the cause of the Spanish flu, the existence of DNA, and the creation of antibiotics.[28] In the COVID crisis, it is profoundly significant that the first pharmaceutical company that managed to develop a vaccine did not accept state subsidies. Moreover, protection against systemic risks during financial crises—a role that has been monopolized by central banks since 1913—used to be provided by private banks that suffered the costs and enjoyed the profits of bailing out selected companies and liquidating others.

Private sector companies fulfill all these roles in competition with one another, and they always have skin in the game. If the

---

27  John M. Barry (2004), *The Great Influenza: The Story of the Deadliest Pandemic in History*, p. 407.

28  John M. Barry, p. 401–418.

private sector is not more involved in the remedy for emergencies, it is because the legislation prohibits it or places great barriers for them being able to do so. After all, all the resources used by the state in crises and emergencies are produced by the private sector; the state, however, claims to be entitled to coordinate the battle against emergencies under a monopoly regime.

Another non-trivial advantage of letting companies provide protection services against crises, rather than the statist approach, would be the prevalence of market prices to guide planning and implementation. No committee of experts can replace the information produced by society as a whole in its interactions through free-market prices. The pricing mechanism, and the disciplining incentives of profit and loss, provide information about how to economize on necessary resources and how to adapt the structure of production to new needs—crucial tasks during an emergency. In the case of the COVID-19 pandemic, shortages of masks appeared in countries that prevented their free trade, production, and distribution. In relatively wealthy European countries like Spain and Austria, where the price of masks was not allowed to reflect their relative scarcity, purchasing masks became a difficult endeavor. In less developed countries like Guatemala or Mexico, the trade and production of masks remained within the free market, and they were as readily available as bread. In cases like this, we observe that the ability to combat the emergency does not depend on the wealth of society as much as having institutional arrangements that allow the provision of important materials through the exercise of entrepreneurship in an environment of free enterprise and competitiveness.

In emergency situations, the exercise of free entrepreneurship, with the spur of competition; the use of scattered, subjective and tacit knowledge, which can be found in free prices; and the set of freedoms and responsibilities that grant skin in the game are crucial for a successful fight against crises without diminishing individual liberties.

One of the most effective ways to fight emergencies without resorting to coercion is through risk-pooling activities. This is one of the most specific ways to use savings and entrepreneurship to limit financial setbacks from harmful chance events such as those that occur in most emergencies. Insurance, specifically, is one of the most notable institutions that human beings have developed to face all those situations that involve risk and uncertainty. It consists of the creation of a pool (from the payment of premiums) that allows the insured party to be compensated in case of suffering a harmful event. This arrangement that allows the reimbursement of the loss suffered by the insured party is known as the elimination of risk.

The use of insurance against crises and emergencies has a series of additional advantages associated with it. The dynamic of the insurance system sets in motion a search for contractual parameters to the insurable event that restrict the actions carried out by the insured party. In competitive markets, restrictions that prove unnecessary will disappear and sensible ones will prove to yield greater profit. Thus, the restrictions set by insurance companies—unlike the case of government protection against emergencies—will tend towards the execution of effective measures and will only involve people who have voluntarily consented. Finally, insurance companies tend to join forces with other insurance companies, via reinsurance contracts in relation to catastrophic risks, to return to normality as soon as possible once the crisis or catastrophic event has taken place.

Insurance is therefore a method for distributing risk among the potentially affected parties of a harmful but uncertain event. It is differentiated from other distribution systems hinging on uncertain events—a bet or wager, for instance—because it uses a "pool" of contributions by various interested parties affected by the same risk. Contributions to this fund are based on the risks associated with each case. In other words, a contribution to the fund depends on the value of the asset to be insured and the probability that the type of damaging event against which it is insured will take place in the specific case that affects the insured assets or persons. It is a mutual hedge of various individual economies affected by the same risk. The insurer limits itself to linking these economies and forming with the total contribution that "pool," or common fund, that transforms an important aspect of uncertainty, related to the risk that is insured, into certainty. This certainty is not achieved by suppressing the event whose associated risk is insured, for it does not directly reduce the possibility of the event occurring. It does not even necessarily reduce—although it could well be the case—the psychological uncertainty related to the occurrence of the damaging event. What it effectively reduces is the uncertainty about the economic impact a certain event may have on the insured party. The certainty provided by the insurance consists in the fact that, in the event of being affected by the harmful event, the insured will have at his disposal a *safe economic value* from the pool that compensates him up to the contracted limit against the economic loss suffered. Creating safety and lessening uncertainty is exactly what is sought with the measures to combat crises. Unfortunately, purchasing insurance against catastrophic or emergency situations is discouraged by the state's interventions—offered "free" and

> **Creating safety and lessening uncertainty is exactly what is sought with the measures to combat crises. Unfortunately, purchasing insurance against catastrophic or emergency situations is discouraged by the state's interventions.**

financed by extracted tax payment when it declares a catastrophic or emergency situation.

## Conclusion

The systematic curtailment of freedoms in the fight against crises and emergencies is a crucial and complex problem, but at the same time, a surmountable one. To allow for an alternative to the statist approach to crises and emergencies, we can rely on a series of measures and institutions that we have at our fingertips.

First of all, we need to encourage entrepreneurship and risk-pooling activities in a cultural environment in which saving is nurtured, competition is welcomed, private property is defended, free trade is fostered, and free prices are respected. This is essential for overcoming the interventionist dynamic that concentrates and accumulates political power at the expense of decentralization and individual freedom and responsibility.

The promotion of a culture of savings makes it possible to stop depending on aid and state intervention during emergencies. Saving alleviates the insecurity associated with uncertainty and provides the essential capital needed in emergency circumstances. Savings can be quickly directed to actions that counter the crisis through private emergency bonds. This savings vehicle enables people to vote with their wallet on the solutions offered. Removing restrictions for entrepreneurs to operate in emergencies, just as they are allowed to operate in international warfare, would help introduce competition and creativity in the fight against crises. Market prices and the profit motive together shed light on the best ways to utilize resources in the creative paths that businessmen may create to fight against crises. Similarly, insurance companies should be able to operate in this sector without restrictions and without facing unfair competition from the state when an emergency or catastrophic situation is declared.

Finally, we must reintroduce checks and balances that would prevent those public officials who declare an emergency from governing during that emergency. This can be very effective in avoiding the unwarranted declaration of emergencies or their renewal, and it reduces the likelihood that "temporary" measures taken in response to a crisis end up becoming permanent.

By carrying out these actions we can aspire to private and voluntary crisis management and bypass the erosion of freedoms that accompanies statist solutions to crises and emergencies.

## Bibliography

Barry, John M. (2004). *The Great Influenza: The Story of the Deadliest Pandemic in History*. USA: Penguin Random House.

Creveld, Martin L. van (1999). *The Rise and Decline of the State*. Cambridge: Cambridge University Press.

Constant, Benjamin (1988). "The effect of illegal and despotic measures on regular governments themselves"; in *Constant, Benjamin. Political Writings*. Edited by and translated by Biancamaria Fontana. Cambridge: Cambridge University Press.

Friedrich, Carl (1968). "Constitutional Dictatorship and Emergency Powers"; in Friedrich, Carl Joachim. *Constitutional Government and Democracy, Fourth Edition*. Waltham: Ginn and Co.

Higgs, Robert (1987). *Crisis and Leviathan: Critical Episodes in the Growth of the State*. Pacific Research Institute.

Huerta de Soto, Jesús (2010). *Socialism, Economic Calculation, and Entrepreneurship*. Cheltenham, UK: Edward Elgar.

Liggio, Leonard P. (1972). "American Foreign Policy and National-Security Managment." Published in *A New History of Leviathan: Essays on the Rise of the American Corporate State*. Edited by Ronald Radosh & Murray N. Rothbard. New York: E.P. Dutton & Co., INC.

Menger, Carl (1892). "On the origin of money." Translated by Caroline A. Foley, *The Economic Journal*, 2(6), p. 239–255

Mises, Ludwig von [1919] (1983). *Nation, State, and Economy. Contributions to the Politics and History of our Time*. Translated by Leland B. Yeager. New York: New York University Press.

Mises, Ludwig von (1918). *Über Kriegskostendeckung und Kriegsanleihen*. Wien: Phoebus.

Mises, Ludwig von (1920). *Die Wirtschaftsrechnung im sozialistischen Gemeinwesen*. Tübingen: Mohr.

Mises, Ludwig von (1922). *Die Gemeinwirtschaft: Untersuchungen über den Sozialismus*. Jena: Verlag von Gustav Fischer.

Mises, Ludwig von (2001). *Crítica del Intervencionismo (El Mito de la Tercera Vía)*. Madrid: Unión Editorial.

Molinari, Gustave de [1849] (1861). "De la Production de la Securité." Published in *Questions D´Économie Politique et De Droit Public*. Brussels: A. Lacroix, Van Meenen Et Cie. Originalmente publicado en *Journal des Economistes*. February 15, 1849.

Molinari, Gustave de (1949[b]). *Les Soirees de la Rue de Saint-Lazare: entretiens sur les lois économiques et défense de la propriété*. Paris: Guillaumin et Cie.

Nozick, Robert (1974). *Anarchy, State and Utopia*. New York: Basic Books.

Ortega y Gasset, José (1926). *La Rebelión de las Masas*. Originally published in a series of newspaper articles in El *Sol*, then in 1930 as a book. Accessed online in 2022 at https://archive.org/details/LaRebelionDeLasMasas/page/n3/mode/2up.

Ortega y Gasset, José (1938). "On Pacifism." *The Nineteenth Century*. July 1938.

Porter, Bruce D. (1994). *War and the Rise of the State. The Military Foundation of Modern Politics*. New York: The Free Press.

Posner, Richard A. (2003). *Law, Pragmatism, and Democracy*. Cambridge: Harvard University Press.

Rossiter, Clinton L. (1948). *Constitutional Dictatorship—Crisis Government in the Modern Democracies*. Princeton: Princeton University Press.

Rothbard, Murray N. (1950). "The Economics of War." Unpublished manuscript.

Rothbard, Murray N. [1970] (1977). *Power and Market: Government and the Economy*. Kansas City: Sheed Andrews and McMeel, Inc.

Rothbard, Murray N. [1962] (1993). *Man, Economy, and State*. Tercera edición. Auburn, Ala.: Ludwig von Mises Institute.

Rothbard, Murray N. (1975). "Society without a State." *The Libertarian Forum* 7 (1): 3–7.

Tilly, Charles (1985). "War Making and State Making as Organized Crime." *Published in Bringing the State Back In*. Peter B. Evans, Dietrich Rueschemeyer and Theda Skocpol (Eds.). Cambridge: Cambridge University Press.

10

# REMEMBERING LEONARD LIGGIO

*Organized by Brad Lips*

---

As discussed in the Introduction to this volume, the annual Liggio Lecture at Atlas Network's Liberty Forum puts a spotlight on an important thought leader, with the goal of enriching the understanding of classical liberalism and inspiring intellectual curiosity among those who follow in this tradition. Another goal—no less important—is to expose this same audience to the personal example of the late Leonard P. Liggio, as a scholar, a movement builder, and a friend.

The 2018 Liggio Lecture by Alex Chafuen, longtime president of Atlas Network who had left the organization the previous year, focused on this latter goal of celebrating Leonard, the person. It's in that spirit that I have assembled the final chapter of this volume.

I include photos, excerpts of letters from friends of Leonard (with their affiliations at the time of Leonard's sixty-fifth birthday), and the text of Leonard's own Presidential Address to the Mont Pelerin Society in 2004. I begin by recounting the broad outlines of Leonard's life, and I give the last word in this book to the late John Blundell and his wife, Christine, who both did so much to celebrate Leonard in his lifetime.

---

*On Leonard's 81st birthday—July 5, 2014—with Brad, Stephanie, and Peter Dylan Lips.*

# Biographical Sketch

Leonard was born on July 5, 1933, in The Bronx, New York. He became a member of Students for Taft upon arriving at Georgetown University and launched a film club on campus that would annually watch *The Fountainhead* at Leonard's behest.

During the 1950s, Leonard encountered some of liberty's heroes of the twentieth century. He sat in on Ludwig von Mises's graduate seminar, attended the meetings of Ayn Rand's "Collective" in her Manhattan apartment, and began a long-running friendship with Murray Rothbard.

He spent nearly sixty years identifying and assisting classical liberal scholars, first as an analyst for the William Volker Fund, and finally—at the time of his death on October 14, 2014—as the executive vice president of Atlas Network.

During his career, he was involved in the founding and early years of celebrated institutions, such as the Intercollegiate Studies Institute (then the Intercollegiate Society of Individualists) and the Institute for Humane Studies (IHS). He had tenures as president of the IHS, the Mont Pelerin Society, and the Philadelphia Society.

He was a beloved teacher, spending decades as a research professor of law at George Mason University, as well as a visiting professor at the Universidad Francisco Marroquin, the Institute for Political and Economic Studies at Georgetown University, and at the University of Aix-en-Provence, France.

He created *Left and Right: A Journal of Libertarian Thought* with Murray Rothbard and George Resch, and later edited *Literature of Liberty: A Review of Contemporary Liberal Thought*. Leonard was a member of the editorial boards of the *Cato Journal* beginning in 1981, of the *American Journal of Jurisprudence* at Notre Dame Law School beginning in 1995, and of *Markets & Morality* beginning in 2000.

*Leonard walks with his friend and collaborator, famed economist Murray Rothbard.*

Leonard was a trustee of the Liberty Fund and the Competitive Enterprise Institute. He also served on the governing boards or advisory boards of the following institutions: the Acton Institute (USA), Centro Interdisciplinar de Ética e Economia Personalista (Brazil), Fundación Burke (Spain), Freda Utley Foundation (USA), Hayek Institute (Austria), Institute for Economic Studies–Europe (France), the Philadelphia Society (USA), The Social Affairs Unit (UK), and Tocqueville Institute (France).

In 2007, he was recognized with the Adam Smith Award, the highest prize bestowed by the Association of Private Enterprise Education. In 2011, he received a Lifetime Achievement Award from the Society for the Development of Austrian Economics.

During his twenty-year tenure at Atlas Network, Leonard inaugurated Atlas Network's important relationship with the John Templeton Foundation by leading The Freedom Project, which established interdisciplinary courses on the nature of freedom at universities in the U.S. and abroad. The Liggio Lecture Series was inaugurated in 2013 as Leonard turned eighty years old, with funding from the Earhart Foundation and Liberty Fund and more than one hundred additional friends of Leonard. Fifteen years prior, Atlas Network published a collection of letters under the title *Born on the 5th of July*, as a celebration of Leonard's sixty-fifth birthday.

# Excerpts of Selected Letters from the *Born on the 5th of July* Tribute to Leonard of 1998

"We know we are a few of the many who seek your counsel, but we are always treated by you, Leonard, as if we were the only ones making demands upon your time and brains. You are a true intellectual missionary. We all love you down here, as we are sure you are loved all over the world."

　—Manuel F. Ayau, Giancarlo Ibárgüen S., Fernando Monterroso V., and Ramon Parellada C., Universidad Francisco Marroquín, Guatemala

"Connecting people of like minds means more to Leonard than graciously introducing them to each other and letting nature take its course. It means, I believe, a commitment to building (or rebuilding) classical liberal thought through young people and across generations by consistently suggesting new, interdisciplinary ways of understanding liberty."

　—Bill Beach, The Heritage Foundation

"Your irrepressible intellectual curiosity and vitality, your enormous energy, your encyclopedic familiarity with scholars in a multitude of fields around the globe, have made you a figure about which some future Liggio-like scholars will surely write, producing, I am confident, a volume that will hearten and inspire future generations of scholars.

　—Israel Kirzner, New York University

*A portrait of Leonard Liggio.*

*Leonard is flanked by American historian Ralph Raico and French economist Henri LePage.*

*Alex Chafuen and Leonard Liggio steered many Atlas Network programs from this office in Fairfax, Virginia.*

*Leonard thumbs through a card catalog drawer at the library of the Institute for Humane Studies.*

"Your commitment to liberty and depth of historical knowledge have been an inspiration and a benefit to generations of libertarians. I remember very fondly your many talks at the late, lamented Cato Institute Summer Seminars. Most of the speakers gave the same talk year after year. But we used to try to trip you up by changing your topic every year, from 'The Role of Ideas in History' to 'The Evolution of Capitalism' to 'Libertarian Ideology in America' to 'Colonialism and Nationalism' to 'Constituencies for Liberty.' Not only were you unfazed by the changes, you amazed us every year by delivering each lecture without notes and with total command of the subject."

—David Boaz, Cato Institute

"I know many of your friends will be sharing their stories about the incessant flow of articles, clippings, books, and emails received from you. Those of us who have the privilege to be close to you, a walking library, are blessed with that same information largesse, but multiplied exponentially. In spending time with you, one sees that you are always ready to lend a helping hand, always willing to spend precious time with friends in pain and friends in joy. Like the Good Samaritan, you are generous also in the way you choose friends."

—Alejandro Chafuen, Atlas Network

"Leonard, I truly admire your indefatigable good spirits and irrepressible optimism that there is a libertarian hidden somewhere in all of us. I doubt that anyone has personally inspired more freedom fighters from more diverse corners of the globe than have you. Being an intellectual mentor to some of the brightest, most committed libertarian scholars in the world must be a source of enormous personal satisfaction to you."

—Ed Crane, Cato Institute

"On behalf of the entire ISI family, I want to convey our heartfelt congratulations to you on the occasion of your sixty-fifth birthday.

"Many are perhaps unaware of the historic connection that exists between you and ISI. Your diligent pursuit of truth, in an age gripped by ideology, took you from your early days at Georgetown College under the mentorship of Charles Callan Tansill, through the Taft years as member of Youth for Taft, and then as a regional director of its successor group, Students for America. An early association with the Foundation (FEE) led to a friendship with Human Events editor and ISI founder Frank Chodorov. Through your association with Chodorov, you founded at Georgetown College in 1953—the year of ISI's founding—the very first ISI college chapter.

"From its very beginnings, then, ISI has been honored by its association with you. As this recital demonstrates, you were literally present at the creation of the conservative movement."

—T. Kenneth Cribb Jr., Intercollegiate Studies Institute

---

"Your counsel and advice, as well as your leadership of the conservative movement in so many areas, has been a real inspiration to me. In the Philadelphia Society, the Mont Pelerin Society, the Acton Institute, ISI, Atlas Network, IHS, and here at Heritage, we have all grown to depend on your sound judgment and keen instinct to do what is both good and what is right."

—Ed Feulner, The Heritage Foundation

---

"I have known and admired you in your capacity as a ferocious but gentle and gracious fighter for freedom. You and others have made much progress in this battle during the past several decades. You should be proud of the impressive achievements."

—Gary Becker, University of Chicago

Leonard Liggio receives a 70th birthday gift organized by John Blundell: a painting of Georgetown as it would have looked during the period of Leonard's undergraduate studies in the early 1950s.

Leonard Liggio assumes the presidency of Mont Pelerin Society at its 2002 General Meeting in London.

*With Walter Grinder, with whom Leonard worked at Institute for Humane Studies to assist and inspire new academics exploring classical liberal ideas.*

*Leonard Liggio at his desk at the Institute for Humane Studies.*

"You taught us that one cannot fully appreciate or understand liberty without a solid grounding in the history of Western Civilization. You taught us the importance not only of intellectual history, which of course is imperative, but also of the millennia of struggles by real individuals and groups of people who fought for their sacred liberties against the mighty forces of state power.

"We learned from you that liberty grew out of the interactions of, inter alia, those perpetual struggles, the thoughts of thousands of minds, both the great and acknowledged as well as the lesser known and forgotten, and the long evolution of liberal institutions. You enlightened us to see that liberalism and individualism, and constitutionalism and federalism did not spring full blown from the writings of theoreticians in eighteenth century Great Britain and America but had their roots deep in the recesses of Western history. For this enriched understanding of liberty and liberalism, I and all the thousands of scholars you have influenced over the years will remain forever grateful.

"I am proud and honored to have you as a continuing mentor and friend."

—Walter Grinder, Institute for Civil Society

"I'm fortunate to have had the opportunity to learn from you, Leonard. First at Institute for Humane Studies after Baldy's death when you stepped up to lead the Institute that you had earlier (Volker Fund days) helped Baldy start. At IHS you introduced me to many scholars, all of whom you knew and whose works you knew extensively. I feel fortunate to have had the same opportunity at Cato and now again at Atlas Network."

—George Pearson, Atlas Network Board Member

"Leonard is a living testament to the truth that one can believe deeply in fundamental individualism and still remain one of the sweetest, kindest, most cooperative and generous people in the world.... Somewhere along the line this man assumed an attitude that we usually think of as properly belonging to religious souls, and we, his legions of friends, are the direct beneficiaries of his good works. The number of organizations that would be floundering today without Leonard's assiduous attention, the number of thankless tasks that no one else could be found to manage, the number of young people who owe their developing careers to his mentoring and ministrations, and the number of friends who have learned to turn to him when a solid shoulder topped by a good brain is needed, these numbers are legion. The details of these episodes could fill volumes. And all of us who have been beneficiaries of Leonard's incredible energy and concern should be very thankful that we have witnessed such rare selflessness."

—Henry Manne, George Mason University School of Law

"I know you have received abundant recognition for your well-deserved reputation as a superb scholar. I wish to take this opportunity to thank you for being a personal friend and mentor. I remember well the first time I met you at 'Camp Cato' during the summer of 1978 at Wake Forest University. It was a wonderful opportunity for me, as a student, to meet others who shared a commitment to the principles of freedom and liberty. You, of course, helped put an excellent academic framework around the many ideas being discussed and debated. Perhaps more important, you took the time to befriend so many of the students. And with so many of us literally running around, I knew that your friendship was individually genuine and personal. You put a genteel human face to the pursuit of truth and liberty."

—Art Pope, Atlas Network Board Member

Leonard spent decades as a research professor of law at George Mason University.

In conversation with Milton Friedman and Swedish MPS member Hakan Gergils.

"Freedom's progress during the last half of the twentieth century has been truly remarkable. It has come from the dedication, sacrifice, and hard work of many people. But as I reflect back over the two decades that I have been involved in this effort, I can think of no one who has played such a unique and vital role in freedom's progress as Leonard Liggio."

—William H. "Chip" Mellor, Institute for Justice

"It is dangerous to have you [Leonard] as a friend—every time I talk to you, you suggest three books I should read. If I ask you to find me copies of them, I then receive them in the mail three days later. Three days after that you ask what I thought of them. Three years later, you will remind me of their arguments. A friendship with you is an education. Most of all, it's a swap of anecdotes and stories and many good laughs."

—Michael Novak, American Enterprise Institute

"No fortune can be more valuable and greater than the friends one has been able to make during his life. You are a rich man, Leonard, and this deserved tribute now makes it evident. You have made friends by the dozens, by the hundreds."

—Donald Stewart, Jr., Instituto Liberal, Brasil

"The Institute for Humane Studies and its students, faculty, and staff have reaped the benefit of your constant efforts to advance a free and humane society. While many get distracted by tertiary issues, you have worked tirelessly with everyone to keep the focus on freedom."

—Charles Koch, Charles Koch Foundation

*Leonard on a conference panel, alongside philosopher and diplomat Michael Novak.*

*Many of us who worked with Leonard, even into the 2000s, remember him using a typewriter... and having a somewhat less tidy desk than in this photo from earlier in his career.*

"Remember what fun—and late-night idea fests—we had in Murray's living room? And the creative meetings with the War Resisters League? You played a key role at Cato in San Francisco. Your work at both IHS and Atlas Network has been inspirational. I love listening to your lectures: each sentence seems to end at a crossroads—you know so much about so many things that you could take any one of a number of fascinating paths to a different field of information."

—Andrea Millen Rich, Center for Independent Thought

"I cannot think what the classical liberal movement would be today were it not for the generosity of this man, of his vocation to be a walking rolodex. He is the indisputable connector of people, ideas, and movements. Numerous books could add his name as co-author, and many more already credit his advice, assistance, and encouragement. Leonard Liggio embodies the adage that there is no limit to what a man can accomplish as long as he doesn't care who gets the credit."

—Rev. Robert A. Sirico, Acton Institute

"Leonard, among the most important of your many contributions may be the leadership that you have provided in carrying the message of freedom to peoples and cultures where liberty has long been compromised or suppressed. In particular, your leadership in articulating the philosophy of freedom to the Muslim and Arab world, and reminding both Muslims and Westerners that limited government, entrepreneurship, and private property have an ancient and a respected pedigree within Islamic civilization, should constitute an inspiration to us all."

—Antony T. Sullivan, The Fund for American Studies

# Presidential Address to the Mont Pelerin Society
# By Leonard P. Liggio
# August 15, 2004

The *London Times Literary Supplement* (June 25, 2004) headlined the lead article: "The Shrinking State" by Lord Skidelsky. Robert Skidelsky is the biographer of Lord Keynes. A TLS subtitle was: "The public domain is disappearing and no political magician can bring it back."

My first reaction is to ask: "What planet is he living on?"

I imagine that if one believes that the State should take 100 percent of income (which was the case for investment income for some time in Great Britain and welfare state countries), then it could be said that the State is shrinking. Compared to the collectivist ideal of complete State control, the current situation is insufficiently perfect.

From the perspective of the collectivist, there has been a decline of the State in the sense that there has been the growth of the private economies in Great Britain and the United States. With the reforms of taxation away from confiscation of property in Great Britain and the United States during the administrations of Margaret Thatcher and Ronald Reagan, productivity and wealth have increased in the past two decades ahead of the tax-collector. The incentives of each person to increase his productivity and provide his customers with a better product at a better price have multiplied. The consumers have benefited, and those serving the consumers have benefited in return. It is a progression very much to be valued.

Great Britain and America have benefited over the past three centuries from similar cycles of tax reduction permitting consumers to benefit from increased productivity.

Although those have not been consistent periods of lower taxes, the succeeding accumulations of capital have permitted progress to resume as taxes later were reduced. The ordinary British or American worker is immensely enriched by the investment of savings in accumulated capital providing the technology to make the worker more productive, from which the worker is rewarded. Millions of poor people have moved to Great Britain and the United States to gain the advantages of the earlier savings and investment in accumulated capital. Continued desire to immigrate is a tribute to the attraction of the rewards to workers of the previous capital accumulation in Great Britain and the United States. Before 1989, no one was crossing the Iron Curtain to enter socialism; the desperate and life-threatening movement was all away from socialism and toward the free society of the West.

It could be that the current increased desire to immigrate is a recognition of the success of Great Britain and the United States in recent capital accumulation. The labor of immigrants is even more rewarded by the recent capital accumulated, saved from taxes.

This situation is a reflection on the failure of other countries to reduce their taxation.

Will the trend toward tax reduction in Great Britain and the United States continue?

Will there be a reversal and a movement toward increasing rates of taxation?

Lord Skidelsky was reviewing the political philosopher David Marquand's *Decline of the Public*. Marquand has given a left-spin so that he includes the government in the "social domain." One should see the social domain as that part of life separated from government—that is, the social domain is the family, private associations, enterprises, religious institutions—those groups which Alexis de Tocqueville identified as distinguishing the modern societies in nineteenth-century Great Britain and America.

Skidelsky sees the original conception of the non-state domain in nineteenth-century English liberalism. The earlier mercantilist system of "patronage, clientism, connection" was replaced by the liberal ideal of merit and reward for performance to the customer. William Gladstone gave form to liberalism. Deriving from the commonwealthmen of the seventeenth century and the Whigs of the eighteenth century, Gladstone's liberalism reduced taxes and government, and insisted on probity in public as well as private relations. Skidelsky sees the "Gladstonian conscience" and private philanthropy as conspicuous features of liberalism. Skidelsky adds: "Marquand offers a left-slanted Whig interpretation of history. He is curiously blind to the religious source of the Gladstonian 'conscience.'"

The "social domain" of Gladstonian liberalism was enlarged by the explosion of the market and the consequent expansion of the middle class. David Green for England and Australia, and David Beito for America, have demonstrated that nineteenth-century liberal society was based in private associations. Of particular significance were the private insurance programs for unemployment and for health. These were rooted in popular fraternities and friendly societies which by the early twentieth century covered most families in England, Australia, and America. David Green and David Beito's books are well worth our reading. They show how these private, fraternal health and unemployment insurance systems were destroyed by state imposed schemes.

In England, the new liberals of David Lloyd George focused on the 10 percent of the population not covered by private health insurance and created a state system to include them. The consequence was the disappearance of the non-tax supported private societies. Similarly, in the United States, the passage by the New Deal of Social Security Act of 1935 was the death knell for the fraternal and friendly societies that included insurance in their services.

Looking at the crisis of the British Welfare State in the 1970s, Skidelsky says: "Academics, puffed up with their specialisms, turned their backs on the public culture, and those who inhabit it. The result was a growing gulf between the suppliers and users of services, and between elites and masses. Market ideology, with its language of producers/providers and customers/clients, offered an alternative model of binding: the invisible hand would make the inefficient and partly corrupt public domain unnecessary."

We are proud of the progress described in Richard Cockett's Thinking the Unthinkable.

We were enthralled by the TV program based on Daniel Yergin and Joseph Stanislaw's *The Commanding Heights: The Battle between Government and the Marketplace that Is Remaking the Modern World* (New York, Simon & Schuster, 1998).

Unnecessary as the Welfare State and the public domain were shown, the Welfare State and its budget has continued to grow both in Great Britain and America. Gladstonian liberalism was rooted in the growth of the middle class, which sold its services in the marketplace where professional competence was judged and rewarded. Instead, the Welfare State has placed the State expert in charge of decisions in place of the consumer. The consumer is replaced by the voter who uses his vote to gain more State resources or to confront the State experts controlling his life. But the voter ends with [others having] more control over his life, more dissatisfaction, and more unsolvable burdens.

Recently, Chancellor of the Exchequer Gordon Brown spoke to the Social Market Foundation (UK) on "A Modern Agenda for Prosperity and Social Reform." Brown described markets as the instruments of "opportunity and security for all." But he added that market failures are so major that state control is necessary, especially in health care and education. Education has been a government industry for a century and a half, and health care in England has been a government industry for more than half a century. Not market failures in health and education, but government failures, over and over again are the reality. Still, the Left insists health care and education must be government industries until the end of time. The more government intervention in health care, the more there is a claim of a health care crisis in the United States. Public education in the United States has been a demonstrable disaster, yet it continues to remain a government industry.

In "The Conversation with [Lord Ralph] Harris and [Arthur] Seldon" (discussed below), Lord Harris says: "State education is one of the most terrible, flawed, failed industries or services in the whole of this nation. There is no way that a private education company could have gone on for a hundred years with a worsening output with every sign of failure, and gone on being funded and funded."

Lord Skidelsky criticizes Marquand:

[H]e underplays the fact that spreading affluence and IT have enormously reinforced the possibilities and attractions of the private, quite apart from any effect of neo-liberal ideology. The era of great issues, whether economic or social, is, for the time being, over.... But it is also partly because Marquand never honestly faces the fact that the intermediate bodies—particularly the professions—long ago surrendered the autonomy which gave them their special role in the Victorian scheme of things by accepting state money.... The universities, whose vanishing independence Marquand stoutly upholds, are the most conspicuous victims of this disastrous evolution.

Lord Skidelsky's attitude gives us the calm feeling of a gradual evolution away from state programs toward market solutions while the free economy produces more affluence. But are not the state's devices for solutions more like those of the Wizard of Oz?

## Presidential Address to the Mont Pelerin Society

A medal instead of courage, a false heart, and a bogus college diploma instead of brains. The Wizard of Oz is the true forerunner of any prime minister of England or any president of the United States in giving bogus health care and bogus education.

The future costs of government pensions and health care for the retired will increase dramatically in coming years, while the number of taxpayers will decline. The crisis is denied by politicians in all countries. Budgets increase for the current year and for the out years in regular acts of self-denial of realistic solutions by legislatures.

The Left talks as though the Welfare State has been repealed. In the United States, each year has seen not only the growth in government spending but enormous new public entitlements that will place larger and larger costs on the budgets. Since the U.S. government has not permitted the calculations to be published, all we know is that the costs will be much beyond the pretended amounts of government statements. Each politician plays the role of King Louis XV's principal mistress, Madame de Pompadour, who declared about royal spending, "After us the Deluge."

Indeed, the consequence of eighteenth-century France's government spending was the debt crisis which culminated in the French Revolution. And as Lady Bracknell said a century ago in Oscar Wilde's *The Importance of Being Ernest*: "I need not remind you of the unfortunate results of that event."

Well, maybe I do need to remind you. The consequences of the accumulation of government debt which resulted in the French Revolution was the Economic Terror in which many were executed for violations of the Law of the Maximum (price controls).

The French National Assembly had confiscated the Church's property to support a paper currency. More and more *Assignats* were printed, causing a runaway inflation fought against by price controls and executions. Napoleon Bonaparte had a popular mandate to end the oppression of Christianity and to restore the gold standard.

Christianity and to restore the gold standard.

All educated Europeans and Americans had the history of the French Revolution engrained in their thinking about public policy. Their commitment to private property, the gold standard and free markets permitted the greatest industrialization in history.

But, during the twentieth century, that memory of the consequences of the debt crisis and the French Revolution dissipated. As George Santayana at Harvard declared: "Those who do not know history are condemned to repeat it."

What is the history which our governments' spending is writing?

Like Madame de Pompadour they are spending money at an escalating rate for future decades. Like her, the politicians proclaim: "After us the Deluge."

There are classical liberal analyses of current developments produced by the numerous public policy research institutes. Institute of Economic Affairs, Centre for Independent Studies, and the North American institutes have provided detailed studies of the growth of the spending of governments. Institutes in other parts of the world have made valuable contributions in their own countries. These are the studies which make the Left declare that the free-market arguments seem dominant in debates regarding public policy.

One of many examples was "The Growth of Government and the Reform of the State in Industrial Countries," by Vito Tanzi and Ludger Schuknecht (IMF Working Papers, December, 1995). *The Economist* headlined its article on the Tanzi-Schuknecht report: "The Withering Away of the State" (April 6, 1996). *The Economist* stated:

For many decades the economic role of the state has grown inexorably.... But perhaps economic history can offer some clues. ... Public spending may be subject to diminishing marginal returns: beyond a certain level, it stops delivering measurable social benefits.

Indeed, as a general rule, those economies with the lowest rise in public spending since 1960 seem to be more efficient and more innovative. They boast lower unemployment and a higher level of registered patents. Moreover, because they do not need to levy high taxes to pay for government largesse, they also tend to have the smallest "black" economies, in which people work but do not pay taxes. ... The authors conclude that rising public spending since 1960 has delivered few social benefits and, in some cases, has hurt economic performance.

Yet, the torrent of current and future entitlements and government spending continues.

The Liberty Fund has produced its "Intellectual Portraits" series of video interviews with major classical liberals. The interview by Stephen Erickson of Pomona College of Ralph Harris and Arthur Selden was published by Institute of Economic Affairs, A Conversation with Harris and Selden (2001). In his Foreword, John Blundell notes: "Ralph Harris often says that in the 1950s talk of markets was akin to swearing in church (particularly when applied to labour markets), yet by 1997 the word 'socialism' did not appear in the Labour manifesto. Is James Buchanan correct when he states, 'Socialism is dead, but Leviathan lives on'? Is Ed Feulner on to something when he asks, 'Can you win the war of ideas but fail to change policy?'"

In the Liberty Fund video, Harris and Seldon explain their classical liberalism in their working class origins. The experts and legislators drawn from the "better classes" doubted the capacity of working class people to act in their own best interests. Out of the kindness of their hearts the elite extend the help of the state to the working class. Seldon says:

> I was appalled by the insensitivity of governments to the efforts of the working classes to help themselves—the belief that they could not do all the necessary things. They were most anxious to ensure that they used all the opportunities of insurance to safeguard their families in times of sickness and loss of work. I began to sense a sort of anti-working class sentiment in all political parties. . . .
> They forgot the history of the working classes. The records are that the working classes were sending their children to school by the 1860s. They were insuring for health coverage and so on by 1910–11 when all parties in England, the main ones Tory and Liberal, with people like Lloyd George and Churchill and Beveridge at the centre, passed the infamous Act of 1911 which forced the working classes to insure with the state, despite the fact that nine-tenths of them were already covered by private systems."

Lord Harris continued:

Arthur said they ignored history. The paradox is that the trade unions had been a major instrument of mutual aid. The unions coming through after the 1850s to 1860s developed philanthropic services: labour exchanges were ways of getting unemployed chaps in their trade into jobs, they developed old-age benefits, they actually developed insurance schemes.

Despite the impressive analyses by institutes, there have not been the over-arching books stating the values of a free society.

Hayek in "The Intellectuals and Socialism" described the strategy of success of the socialists. Their scholarly works set forth the values of a command society. They became the framework for the essayists and journalists to write about current events. The widespread acceptance of the assumptions of government intervention permitted left journalists to write unchallenged regarding issues.

From Hayek's *The Road to Serfdom* there was a period of active challenge to the growth of the Welfare State. Classical liberal scholars wrote classics which we gratefully study. The many tens of millions who died in the Soviet Gulags and Mao's labor camps were reminders of the growth of the state. Today are we so comfortable that we need not concern ourselves with long-term prospects? Will we be like Bishop Talleyrand? He escaped the Terror by roughing it a short time in America and declared: "No one who did not live before the French Revolution can imagine how comfortable life was."

Where are today's scholarly products of classical liberal scholarship? Do classical liberals lack the incentives that there is not an immediate threat to "our lives, our fortunes and our sacred honor"? Is our immediate situation so comfortable that there is no motivation to challenge opposing systems of ideas?

Think of the classical liberals who are members (or not) of the Mont Pelerin Society. Can we feel confident that the intellectual power that existed in the past is continuing? At the last general meeting of the Mont Pelerin Society, organized in London by John Blundell, we had the immense pleasure of hearing that the Swedish Nobel Committee in Economic Science had awarded the 2002 prize to Vernon Smith of George Mason University. We can think of several members who deserve the Nobel Prize. But I do wonder about the future beyond them.

Economics is not the only discipline in which classical liberalism does not appear to be producing distinguished work. Perhaps it is the problem of specialization. In order to achieve tenure and promotion, scholars must produce to the narrow demands of their departments. Their focus is aimed below the horizon. Lots of small pieces do not add up to widely read contributions. Similarly, such work must be non-controversial. Safety in the ordinary can mean work that stays below a higher radar screen.

Many persons are doing fine work which I appreciate. But few are making an impact.

I can think of very important work in economics by Robert Barro, Deepak Lal, Roland Vaubel, and Bruno Frey; in law by Richard Epstein and Randy Barnett; in American social history by David Beito; in political philosophy by Anthony de Jasay and Chandran Kukathas; on private education and the poor by James Tooley. Their work properly has received wide attention. The Harvard historian Richard Pipes's *Property and Freedom* and Fareed Zakaria's *The Future of Freedom* have been valuable contributions. The books and the hands-on work of Hernando de Soto (winner of the 2004 Friedman Prize for Liberty) has been spectacular. The work of few others now has received the wide attention which the work of George Gilder and Charles Murray received two decades ago.

I fear that classical liberals are shrinking as a scholarly force before the intellectual public.

I think that it is valuable for us to look around us and consider the present and the future.

Where will the future classical liberal scholars come from if we see fewer of them making a mark today?

Do we know whether the new technology will have an impact? If academic specialization has detached scholars from the educated public, is there emerging a new public humanities?

What were the sources of classical liberal scholarship in the 1950s and 1960s that produced so many stars? Who were the personalities and the institutions that attracted young scholars to become classical liberal leaders?

It is our duty to address the questions of what were the sources of classical liberal scholarship in the 1950s and 1960s, and what were the personalities and institutions that had attracted young scholars to become classical liberal leaders. We do not want classical liberalism to calmly fade into the sunset.

30th June 1998

Professor Leonard P Liggio
Executive Vice President
Atlas Economic Research Foundation
4084 University Drive, Suite 103
Fairfax
VA 22030-6812
USA

# iea
The Institute of
Economic Affairs

2 Lord North Street
London SW1P 3LB
Telephone: +44 (0)171 799 3745
Facsimile: +44 (0)171 799 2137
E-mail: iea@iea.org.uk
Internet: http://www.iea.org.uk

Dear Leonard,

What can we say about the man who used to drive Ayn Rand right up the wall? You drove her totally mad, not by disagreeing with her, but rather by falling asleep on her sofa!

How easy it is to visualise: Murray Rothbard wide awake and taking it all in; Joey Rothbard banished to the kitchen to read aetheist tracts; and you Leonard fast asleep on the sofa!

But what heady days in your youth, to be there when the first box of *Atlas Shrugged* landed in New York, to work for Taft, to help found ISI (the Intercollegiate Society of Individualists note), to know von Mises and his circle and to help FA "Baldy" Harper set up IHS.

We're told that in the 'sixties some libertarians wore buttons bearing the words "Murray knows everything" while others wore ones that read "And Leonard knows the rest". You and John were browsing together in a New York bookstore in 1975 when John pointed excitedly to the new Rothbard book *Conceived In Liberty, Volume 1 : A New Land, A New People - The American Colonies in the Seventeenth Century*. Had you seen this new book, John asked? You smiled, picked up the book, opened it to the title page and pointed to the by-line. It read not "Murray Rothbard" but rather "Murray Rothbard with the assistance of Leonard P Liggio" and in the Preface of this volume and also volumes II, III and IV we read:

> "But my greatest debt is to Leonard P Liggio, of City College, CUNY, whose truly phenomenal breadth of knowledge and insight into numerous fields and areas of history are an inspiration to all who know him. Liggio's help was indispensable in the writing of this volume, in particular his knowledge of the European background."

Many, many books have seen the light of day with the assistance of Leonard P Liggio. Many, many young careers have soared with the assistance of Leonard P Liggio. And many, many minds have been steered to more productive pastures with the assistance of Leonard P Liggio.

Thank you for everything.

Chris

**Christine V Blundell**
Director
Student Programmes

John

**John Blundell**
General Director

P.S. We've never believed this business about your date of birth being July 5th. If ever a man was meant to be born on the 4th it is you.

Registered office
Registered No. 755502
Charity No. CC/235 351
Limited by Guarantee

# About Atlas Network

Atlas Network is a non-profit organization, based in Arlington, Virginia, that aims to secure for all individuals the rights to economic and personal freedom.

Founded in 1981 by think tank pioneer Sir Antony Fisher, Atlas Network has a global vision of a free, prosperous, and peaceful world where the principles of individual liberty, property rights, limited government, and free markets are secured by the rule of law.

Atlas Network's vision is best achieved by independent think tanks with the local knowledge to be effective agents of change, prioritizing institutional increases in freedom that can improve opportunities for vast numbers of people.

To accelerate the pace of achievement by its partners in their communities, Atlas Network implements programs within its Coach, Compete, Celebrate™ strategic model.

Atlas Network is not endowed and accepts no government funding. It depends on private philanthropy to carry out its annual programs, which includes awarding seed funding for more than one hundred of the most promising projects developed by its partners.

Learn about how you can get involved at AtlasNetwork.org.

ATLAS NETWORK